The Electronic Front Porch

MERCER
UNIVERSITY PRESS

Endowed by
TOM WATSON BROWN
and
THE WATSON-BROWN FOUNDATION, INC.

The Electronic Front Porch

An Oral History of the Arrival of Modern Media in Rural Appalachia and the Melungeon Community

Jacob J. Podber

Mercer University Press

Macon, Georgia

MUP/H475

© 2007 Mercer University Press
1400 Coleman Avenue
Macon, Georgia 31207
All rights reserved

First Edition.

Books published by Mercer University Press are printed on acid free paper that meets the requirements of American National Standard for Information Sciences—Permanence of Paper for Printed Library Materials.

Library of Congress Cataloging-in-Publication Data

ISBN 978-0-88146-089-6

Podber, Jacob J.
The electronic front porch : an oral history of the arrival of modern media in rural Appalachia and the Melungeon community / Jacob J. Podber. –1st ed. p. cm.
Includes bibliographical references and index.
ISBN-13: 978-0-88146-089-6 (hardback : alk. paper)
ISBN-10: 0-88146-089-3 (hardback : alk. paper)
1. Mass media—Social aspects—Appalachian Region.
2. Internet—Social aspects—Appalachian Region.
3. Melungeons— Effect of technological innovations on—Appalachian Region. 4. Popular culture—Appalachian Region—History—20th century. 5. Appalachian Region—Social conditions—20th century. 6. Appalachian Region—Social conditions—21st century. I. Title.
HN79.A127P63 2007
302.23089'050755—dc22
2007019736

In memory of Yankel Podberesky

**Merry Christmas, Love, and Kisses,
From Rachel (and Jake)**

The Melungeons

Sometimes called "Melungeons," the earliest nonnative "Americans" to live in Appalachia were—perhaps—of Mediterranean extraction and of a Jewish or Muslim religious persuasion. For fear of discrimination–since "persons of color" were often disenfranchised and abused–the Melungeons were reticent regarding their heritage. In fact, over time, many Melungeons themselves "forgot" where they came from. Hence, today, Melungeons remain the "last lost tribe in America," even to themselves. Once lost, but now, forgotten no more. This series explores the origins, history, and culture of these once-forgotten people.

—Wayne Winkler , series editor
—N. Brent Kennedy, founding editor

Contents

Illustrations

Foreword

The Electronic Front Porch is an interdisciplinary work that examines the arrival of radio, television, and the Internet in rural Appalachia. In addition to media and Appalachian scholars, the audience for this book includes readers interested in issues dealing with popular culture; class; and oral, Southern, and American history. Although each chapter is designed to interlink, the book is written to allow readers to concentrate on any specific topic, while skipping others until a later time.

In the introduction to *The Electronic Front Porch*, titled "Identity and the Researcher as Participant," I examine issues surrounding both the formation of group identity as well as my relationship with the participants in this study. The next four chapters contextualize the body of the study in different ways. Chapter 1, "The Study of Media," is a general introduction to media studies. Chapter 2, "Uncovering Oral History," presents a primer on oral history interviewing methodology. Chapter 3, "Appalachia on My Mind: Outsiders' Construction of Appalachian Identity," provides a general overview of Appalachian history as well as an introduction to Appalachian Studies. Chapter 4, "Melungeon Construction of Identity," introduces the reader to the Melungeon community of Appalachia. Chapters 5, 6, and 7 examine the arrival in rural Appalachia of radio, television, and the Internet, respectively, and the effects on the residents of the region. Lastly, Chapter 8 is a summary of my findings along with concluding remarks that provide links to larger issues surrounding the future of electronic media.

In addition, Appendix A provides the reader with a list of each participant, his or her birthplace, and date of birth. In Appendix B, the reader will find questions used during my oral history interviewing process.

Acknowledgments

There are countless people deserving of my thanks and appreciation who have made invaluable contributions to this book. First and foremost, I would like to thank Rachel Stocking for her insightful comments and suggestions, unwavering support, and never-ending encouragement.

As an assistant professor in the Radio-Television Department at Southern Illinois University Carbondale, I have been the grateful recipient of grants that supported my research, including those from the SIUC Office of Research and Development Administration and the SIUC College of Mass Communication and Media Arts. The support of my colleagues, including my dean, Manjunath Pendakur, and department chairpersons, Phylis Johnson and John Downing, has been invaluable.

Frank Chorba, editor of the *Journal of Radio Studies*, in which earlier material from this book first appeared, has given me help and friendship throughout the years. In addition, heartfelt thanks go to Patrick Murphy and Marwan Kraidy, editors of the book *Global Media Studies: Ethnographic Perspectives*, in which previous material from this manuscript was first published as a book chapter. Keith Witt, Geographic Information Specialist at the Appalachian Regional Commission, was generous with his assistance in providing cartographic maps for this book. Special thanks also go to David Mould, a valued advisor throughout graduate school, who supervised my first research in Appalachia and directed my dissertation.

Finally, I would like to thank the people of Appalachia who shared their stories with me. Without their voices, this book would not have been possible.

Introduction

Identity and the Researcher as Participant

Through the use of oral histories, this book looks at how the arrival of radio, television, and the Internet affected the lives of people in rural Appalachia. Starting with radio's inception in the 1920s and 1930s, followed by television's arrival in the 1950s and 1960s, and ending with the current expansion of the Internet, I look at participants' memories of each medium, how they used it, and the impact electronic media had on their lives.

Interpretive researchers have been criticized for attempting to speak "for" a group of people. Some researchers claim that their studies will give a "voice" to a particular group. This mistakenly assumes that the group being studied had no voice before the arrival of the researcher. Some have observed that within the Appalachian region, outsiders first appropriated land, then natural resources, and they are now appropriating its culture.

In "The Appalachian Inheritance," Cattell-Gordon describes the Appalachian region as a "culturally transmitted traumatic stress syndrome."[1] By comparison, Banks, Billings, and Tice suggest that:

> This account of the effects of history as social trauma bred in the bones of the people of the region is flawed because it constitutes Appalachians solely as "victims" and obscures the potentiality of diverse subjects making history...thereby minimizing

---

[1] David Cattell-Gordon, "The Appalachian Inheritance: A Culturally Transmitted Traumatic Stress Syndrome?" *Journal of Progressive Human Services* 1/1 (1990): 41.

the possibilities for agency and empowerment. Such an account leaves unquestioned paradigmatic views of Appalachia that have the effect of either marginalizing and excluding Appalachians as fully human beings or else treating them as a monolithic category.[2]

By using oral histories, my intention is to give an outlet to residents of rural Appalachia. Using their words, I hope to show how they define their identity, how their use of electronic media has informed that identity, and how they have been included and excluded by electronic media. This book records participants' lived, reconstructed, and/or perceived pasts.

While traveling around Appalachia, recording the life stories of interviewees, I recognized that it was the inception of radio in the 1920s—and, for some, television several decades later—that reaffirmed a sense of belonging to a national community for this region of the country. As Hilmes observes, "Radio seemed in its early days to lend itself to association with ideas of nation, of national identity, to the heart and mind of America."[3]

Because of their geographical isolation, some rural communities appeared to have much to gain from early electronic media. With the arrival of radio, especially in the 1930s with high-powered clear channel stations that broadcast from the "big city," listeners in the most isolated regions of the country felt, as Smulyan observed, connected with the rest of the world.[4] By listening to newscasts on the radio, they learned how others coped with the Great Depression and shared the pain, losses, and victories of World War II with other listeners around the country. Daily soap operas allowed radio listeners to learn "of critical values, of

---

[2] Alan Banks, Dwight Billings, and Karen Tice, "Appalachian Studies and Postmodernism," in *Multicultural Experiences, Multicultural Theories*, ed. Mary Rogers et al. (New York: McGraw-Hill, 1996) 82.

[3] Michele Hilmes, *Radio Voices: American Broadcasting, 1922–1952* (Minneapolis: University of Minnesota Press, 1997) 1.

[4] Susan Smulyan, *Selling Radio: The Commercialization of American Broadcasting 1920–1934* (Washington: Smithsonian Institution Press, 1994).

themselves, and of their fellow citizens. The premise of all soaps was the commonness of the American experience."[5]

On the other hand, Riesman offered an alternative view of the effects of electronic media on our sense of community in his "lonely crowd" theory.[6] His analogy of the individual living in a modern technological society yet existing in seclusion seems to convey the belief that electronic media are isolating catalysts on society. The analysis of this question—whether the arrival of electronic communication technology in Appalachia disrupted rather than enhanced senses of community—defines this study.

Although much has been written on the coal mining communities of Appalachia,[7] and on ethnicity within the region,[8] there is a dearth of literature on electronic media usage in the area. An important distinction should be made in that there is a body of work that examines print media's effect on Appalachia.[9] In addition, Newcomb[10] and Harkins[11]

---

[5] Fred J. MacDonald, *Don't Touch that Dial! Radio Programming in American Life, 1920–1960* (Chicago: Nelson-Hall, 1979) 239.

[6] David Riesman, *The Lonely Crowd: A Study of the Changing American Character* (New Haven: Yale University Press, 1950).

[7] See Stephen L. Fisher, *Fighting Back in Appalachia: Traditions of Resistance and Change* (Philadelphia: Temple University Press, 1993); Mike Yarrow, "Voices From the Coalfields," in *Communities in Economic Crisis: Appalachia and the South*, ed. John Gaventa, Barbara E. Smith, and Alex W. Willingham (Philadelphia: Temple University Press, 1990) 38–52; Ronald Eller, *Miners, Millhands, and Mountaineers: Industrialization of the Appalachian South, 1880–1930* (Knoxville: University of Tennessee Press, 1982).

[8] See William Hobart Turner and Edward J. Cabbell, *Blacks in Appalachia* (Lexington: University Press of Kentucky, 1985); James Klotter, "The Black South and White Appalachia," *Journal of American History* 66/4 (March 1980): 832–49; Rodger Cunningham, "Scotch-Irish and Others," *Appalachian Journal* 18/1 (Fall 1990): 84–90; Bob Snyder, "Image and Identity in Appalachia," *Appalachian Journal* 9/2 (Winter/Spring 1982): 124–33.

[9] Lowndes Stephens, "Media Exposure and Modernization among the Appalachian Poor," *Journalism Quarterly* 49/2 (Summer 1972): 247–57; Sally Maggard, "Cultural Hegemony: The News Media and Appalachia," *Appalachian Journal* 12/3 (Autumn/Winter 1984-85): 67–83.

[10] Horace Newcomb, "Appalachia on Television: Region as Symbol of American Popular Culture," *Appalachian Journal* 7/1-2 (Autumn/Winter 1979-80): 155-64.

examine how Appalachian stereotypes are perpetuated on TV, Williamson points out how the Appalachian is portrayed in motion pictures,[12] and some alternative media sources, such as Appalshop Film and Video in Whitesburg, Kentucky, produce works on Appalachian culture and history.[13] None, however, address electronic media usage by Appalachians. The oral histories collected in this study contribute to an understanding of the impact radio, television, and the Internet have had on the residents of rural Appalachia by creating a human diary that documents how early listeners and viewers chose their radio and television programs; how, where, and with whom they listened and watched; and perhaps most importantly, how electronic media affected their lives. Similarly, the oral histories used to trace the early adoption of the Internet contribute to a better understanding of how Melungeons, a community in rural Appalachia that historically has been perceived as "other," were able to use electronic media to establish communities—both virtually and in real life—regardless of their geographical isolation.[14]

---

[11] Anthony A. Harkins, "The Hillbilly in the Living Room: Television Representations of Southern Mountaineers in Situation Comedies, 1952-1971." *Appalachian Journal* 29/1-2 (Fall/Winter 2001-2002): 98–126. Also see Anthony A. Harkins, *Hillbilly: A Cultural History of an American Icon* (New York: Oxford University Press, 2004).

[12] See Jerry Wayne Williamson, *Southern Mountaineers in Silent Films: Plot Synopses of Movies about Moonshining, Feuding, and Other Mountain Topics, 1904–1929* (Jefferson NC: McFarland, 1994) and *Hillbillyland: What the Movies Did to the Mountains and What the Mountains Did to the Movies* (Chapel Hill: University of North Carolina Press, 1995).

[13] Created in 1969 as a War on Poverty program to train young people in media production, Appalshop is a media arts center located in central Appalachia where it continues to produce and present works on social, economic, and political issues concerning Appalachian culture. For example, see *Mountain Vision: Homegrown Television in Appalachia*, videocassette, directed by Susan Wehling and Jeff Hawkins (Whitesburg, KY: Appalshop, 1990) and *Strangers and Kin*, videocassette, directed by Herb E. Smith (Whitesburg KY: Appalshop, 1984).

[14] The second edition of *Webster's Dictionary* describes a Melungeon as "a member of a dark-skinned people of mixed Caucasian, Negro, and Indian stock, inhabiting the Tennessee mountains." There is, however, a great deal of mythology surrounding Melungeon identity. For instance, one legend contends that the original

Researcher as Participant

This project is a qualitative study on early electronic media usage in rural Appalachia. Since reflexivity is a vital element in qualitative studies, it is important to examine my own identity as a researcher and my relationship to the participants in this study.

In the Broadway musical, *A Chorus Line*, the Latin-American character, Morales, points out that she didn't change her name because she figured "ethnic was in."[15] With the arrival of the new millennium, the winner of an award for best writer at the 2000 Emmy Award Ceremony addressed how remarkable it was that his mother and father had escaped Nazi Germany and years later he was receiving an award for writing a television show about the United States political scene (*The West Wing*). Another writer that evening proudly announced his gayness to hundreds of millions of viewers worldwide when receiving his Emmy Award. Today, everything from soda pop to MP3 players are marketed via mainstream media outlets using hip-hop culture. In fact, young white suburban males make up a large market for hip-hop music. Suddenly, among many groups who do not have a strong ethnic identity (other than white), it is hip to be the "other" in the United States. Groups that were historically marginalized and persecuted now proudly announce their identity. Brodkin addresses how in post-World War II America, "white America embraced Jews and even Jewishness as part of itself.... Jews could become Americans and Americans could be like Jews, but Israel and the Holocaust set limits to assimilation."[16] However, this limit appears to have lessened over the past half century as the winner of an Emmy invokes the memory of the Holocaust and the wife of the 2000 Democratic vice-presidential candidate speaks of being a child of

---

Melungeons were escaped slaves or mutineers from African/Portuguese boats that jumped ship while approaching the Southeastern seaboard of North America and fled to the Tennessee mountains to hide. For a detailed discussion of Melungeon identity construction, see chapter 4.

[15] James Kirkwood and Nicholas Dante, *A Chorus Line* (New York: Applause, 1975) 28.

[16] Karen Brodkin, *How Jews Became White Folks: And What That Says about Race in America* (New Brunswick NJ: Rutgers University Press, 1998) 140.

Holocaust survivors. Each appears to be appealing to something in all Americans. Perhaps the American ideal of assimilation and of the melting pot goes against humankind's need to belong to a tribe—that is, to be simultaneously a member of a group and yet to remain uniquely different from everyone else. Advertisers have long recognized this trend. Bennetton ads are not so much about the clothes they sell as about how cool it is to be ethnic. The issue of identity and being "the other" was at the forefront of my thinking when I embarked upon this project.

Lynch observes that reflexivity "is an unavoidable feature of the way actions (including actions performed, and expressions written, by academic researchers) are performed, made sense of and incorporated into social settings."[17] In participant-observation, reflexivity has become a major component as textbooks often instruct students to examine their relationship to the groups they study.[18] In fact, some argue that the removal of the researcher from the text is a shortcoming. Sultana observes that "it is because the researcher edits himself/herself out of the text that we often get so little information on such details as the researcher's expectations and presuppositions, or the surprises that were encountered in the field."[19] In *Life in Big Red*, Conquergood is as much a participant in the text as are the participants he discusses.[20] As

---

[17] Michael Lynch, "Against Reflexivity as an Academic Virtue and Source of Privileged Knowledge," *Theory, Culture & Society* 17/3 (June 2000): 26.

[18] R. F. Ellen, ed., *Ethnographic Research: A Guide to General Conduct* (London: Academic Press, 1992); Martin Hamersley and Paul Atkinson, *Ethnography: Principle in Practice* (London: Tavistock, 1983).

[19] Ronald Sultana, "Ethnography and the Politics of Absence," in *Critical Theory and Educational Research* (Albany: State University of New York Press 1995) 116–17.

[20] Dwight Conquergood, "Life in Big Red: Struggles and Accommodations in a Chicago Polyethnic Tenement," in *Structuring Diversity: Ethnographic Perspectives on the New Immigration*, ed. Louise Lamphere (University of Chicago Press, 1992) 95–144. Also see Crystal Wilkinson, "On Being 'Country': One Affrilachian Woman's Return Home," in *Confronting Appalachian Stereotypes: Back Talk from an American Region*, ed. Dwight B. Billings, Gurney Norman, and Katherine Ledford (Lexington: University Press of Kentucky, 1999) 184–86; Stuart Hall, "Who Needs Identity?," in *Questions of Cultural Identity*, ed. Stuart Hall and P. Du Gay (London: Sage, 1996) 1–17; Stephen L. Fisher, "Appalachian Stepchild," in *Confronting Appalachian Stereotypes: Back Talk from an American Region*, ed. Dwight B. Billings,

Fleischman observes, ethnographers must somehow incorporate themselves into the study.[21] However, Fine examines the importance of the relationship between the researcher and the participants as she refers to working the hyphen between insider and outsider.[22] In addition, Collins addresses conditions related to being an "outsider within."[23] To be honest, while conducting my research in Appalachia, I always felt like an insider in outsider's clothing.

Having grown up in Atlanta, Georgia, the son of Holocaust survivors, I still think of myself as a southerner even though I have lived most of my adult life in New York, London, and Los Angeles. Upon relocating to Appalachian Ohio to begin research on this book, I was surprised by the ease I felt sharing yarns with my new neighbors. While their accents sounded a bit different from the Georgian accents of my youth, many Appalachians I met reminded me of my childhood neighbors. As colleagues flew to Africa and Turkey to pursue their media research agendas, I recognized that the rural community in which I lived was filled with important stories on the impact early electronic media had on rural communities.

Of course, I recognize that as a white urbanite male doing interpretive research within a marginalized group, I might raise some eyebrows. There is some discussion within the academy as to whether it is even possible for an "outsider" to record a community's history

---

Gurney Norman, and Katherine Ledford (Lexington: University Press of Kentucky, 1999) 187–90; Fred Hobson, "Up in the Country," in *Confronting Appalachian Stereotypes: Back Talk from an American Region*, ed. Dwight B. Billings, Gurney Norman, and Katherine Ledford (Lexington: University Press of Kentucky, 1999) 174–86.

[21] Suzanne Fleischman, "Gender, the Personal and the Voice of Scholarship: A Viewpoint," *Signs: Journal of Women in Culture and Society* 23/4 (Summer 1998): 975–1016.

[22] Michelle Fine, "Working the Hyphens: Reinventing Self and Other in Qualitative Research," in *Handbook of Qualitative Research*, ed. Norman K. Denzin and Yvonna S. Lincoln (Thousand Oaks: Sage Publications, 1994) 70–82.

[23] P. H. Collins, "Learning from the Outsider Within: The Sociological Significance of Black Feminist Thought," in *(En)Gendering Knowledge: Feminists in Academe*, ed. Joan Hartman and Ellen Messer-Davidow (Knoxville: The University of Tennessee Press, 1991) 40–65.

effectively. There is perhaps a danger of swinging toward a totally inclusive expectation for research. Gluck and Patai address "research by, about, and for women."[24] African-American Studies departments often have few majors who are not of color. As Kipling wrote, "What should they know of England who only England know?"[25] So who was I to think that I could go into rural Appalachian communities and extract significant oral histories?

Growing up in Atlanta made me southern, but this did not make me an Appalachian. In fact, as I examine in chapter 3, defining Appalachia is a task that many might say is unachievable. As I conducted interviews within Appalachia, my own feelings of belonging to a "marginal" group would often resurface. This was especially the case while interviewing Melungeons in northeast Tennessee, southwest Virginia, and beyond.

Religion should be personal, a covenant between oneself and one's God. I believe this to be true, but I cannot help but think that I was somehow conditioned by my family not to publicize my otherness. Even before the yellow Star of David became the vogue in Nazi-occupied Europe, blatant attestation to one's Jewishness was often hazardous. To survive in this hostile epoch, some learned to make their Jewishness less visible. I believe this is part of the legacy that was passed on to the next generation.

I cannot recall a single incident in my childhood of blatant anti-Semitism. It was not until my freshman year at college that I recall my first salvo. Sitting in my dorm with several Jewish-American friends, the door to my room burst open and in walked the resident assistant. Looking around the room he bellowed, "Hey, let's all go fly a kike!" Having never before heard the word "kike" used in a complete sentence, my response was to break out into uncontrollable laughter. Fortunately, this seemed to disarm the attacker who never again said anything quite as humorous. My friends, however, did not find the incident so amusing and were noticeably upset by my reaction. What immediately came to

---

[24] Sherna Berger Gluck and Daphne Patai, *Women's Words: The Feminist Practice of Oral History* (New York: Routledge, 1991) 2.

[25] Rudyard Kipling, "The English Flag," in *Extravagant Strangers: A Literature of Belonging*, ed. Caryl Phillips (Boston: Faber and Faber, 1997) 37.

mind was a radio interview I had heard with author Jerzy Kosinski. Having survived the Holocaust as a child, he spoke of hiding from the Germans under the pillows of a sofa. It was necessary for him to become invisible. To a certain extent, that is what happened to me that day in my dorm room. Unlike some Melungeons to whom I spoke who could not, even if they chose to, hide their telltale physical attributes, I could become an invisible Jewish-American.

When I lived in New York City, where it could be argued that in certain neighborhoods the "other" is the "non-Jewish-American," I would spend my summer weekends on Long Island. Given the expense of beach rentals, it was necessary for up to twenty people to share a house. Ten relative strangers would crowd into a beach bungalow on alternate summer weekends. Spending every other weekend in such close quarters quickly turned relative strangers into intimate friends. On my last weekend at the beach, I was seated next to a housemate named Melissa. Around her neck, I noticed a gold necklace with the name "Shoshana" inscribed in Hebrew. Given that the English translation for Shoshana is Susan, I asked Melissa why her English name did not match her Hebrew name. Dumbfounded, she looked at me and asked how I was able to read Hebrew. She had no idea that I was Jewish. I took some pleasure in the fact that someone could live with me for ten weekends and not know I was Jewish. However, a feeling of remorse soon swept over me. My legacy had served me, but to what end? I may have been an invisible Jewish-American, but at a higher price than I felt comfortable paying. How I longed not to be the "other."

As I grew up speaking English with a southern drawl at school, Yiddish was the language spoken at home. That is, until my parents received a call from the principal of my elementary school. It seemed my older brother was appropriating Yiddish words into his vocabulary. He told a bully that if he did not watch out, the bully would get a "potch" across his face. The beauty of Yiddish is its rich usage of onomatopoeia. However, the bully was unfamiliar with the term and as a result was unable to understand that my brother was threatening him with a "slap." As with many confrontations, what started out as a mere misunderstanding escalated into a fight. When my parents arrived at the principal's office, there appeared to be more concern over the fact that my brother was not speaking English than there was over the altercation. Convinced that my brother would not be able to communicate his future defensive threats unless my parents stopped speaking Yiddish at home, the Atlanta public school authorities intimidated my parents into giving up the language that Hitler, Germany, and the Third Reich could not. As my parents struggled with English in the privacy of their home, I realized that I was being deprived of another part of my legacy. Anzaldua tells of her teacher saying, "If you want to be American, speak 'American.' If you don't like it, go back to Mexico where you belong."[26] A similar threat to my parents would have meant a return to a hell that probably no one in the Atlanta public school system could even imagine. That explicit threat was never made but the exhortation to speak only English was an attack on their form of expression with the intent to censor. In speaking with Melungeon participants (see chapter 4), some recalled being told to go back "where you belong," although these admonitions created a slight bit of confusion in that a number of participants could trace their ancestry back to the American Revolutionary War.

While a child in the late 1950s, my father took me to the Atlanta Farmers' Market to purchase vegetables for his grocery store. Joe, the African-American butcher who worked with my father, met us there to help transport the produce. After our vehicles were loaded, my father asked if I wanted to have breakfast at the market. When I said yes, my father turned to Joe and told him we would all meet back at the parking lot in thirty minutes. With that, Joe walked off. I asked my father why Joe was not joining us. He replied that he must not be hungry. I called out for Joe, but he kept walking. I knew I was somehow in the middle of an embarrassing lie. It was not until years later that I realized the Atlanta Farmers' Market had segregated dining rooms. Throughout this project, whenever I would think back to my childhood in Atlanta, much of what made up my retrospection of the South was not necessarily the sunbelt

---

[26] Gloria Anzaldua, "How to Tame a Wild Tongue," in *Out There: Marginalization and Contemporary Cultures*, ed. Russell Ferguson, Martha Gever, Trinh T. Minh-Ha, and Cornel West (Cambridge: MIT Press, 1990) 203.

that rises in stature to symbolize American cultural and economic progress,[27] but the South of the Atlanta Farmers' Market.

While conducting interviews for this book, the line between insider and outsider was not always clear to me. When Melungeons spoke of feelings of being the "other," I would want to tell stories similar to the ones above. When participants spoke of wanting to identify with characters on television, I had palpable childhood recollections of wishing I lived in "Springfield" with a brother named "Bud" and sisters with names like "Princess" and "Kitten." In *Do I Like Them Too Much?": Effects of the Oral History Interview on the Interviewer and Vice-Versa*, Yow addresses the importance of not allowing personal feelings toward the interviewee to affect the line of questioning an oral historian pursues or addresses.[28] However, I do not believe I would have gotten the heartfelt stories I did had I not strongly identified with those who participated in this project.

---

[27] Ronald Eller, foreword to *Confronting Appalachian Stereotypes: Back Talk from an American Region*, ed. Dwight B. Billings, Gurney Norman, and Katherine Ledford (Lexington: University Press of Kentucky, 1999).

[28] Valerie Yow, "Do I Like Them Too Much?: Effects of the Oral History Interview on the Interviewer and Vice-Versa," *The Oral History Review* 24/1 (Summer 1997): 55–79.

Chapter One

The Study of Media

Plato considered the perfect size of a politically responsible city to have a population no greater than the number of people who could hear the voice of an orator. The invention of the printing press (not to mention the telegraph, telephone, radio, television, and the Internet) made Plato's observation more than archaic. The development of new communications technology has changed the way the world operates. However, although the history of media has largely been driven by new technology, the effects of those technologies on communities are unintelligible without looking at their social, cultural, political, and economic contexts.

Media in its Social Context

One might say that the study of media history and its social contexts begins with the analysis of the Ten Commandments. The second commandment, "Thou shalt not make unto thee any graven images," guided the Hebrews away from the visual arts and toward the "Word." Postman argues that Moses was wise to choose writing as the mode to objectify an unseeable god.[1] Writing, after all, is a method of using symbols to convey symbols. What better way to describe a non-material god, especially for a group of people about to wander around the desert

---

[1] Neil Postman and Camille Paglia, "Two Cultures—Television Versus Print," in *Communication in History: Technology, Culture, Society*, ed. David Crowley and Paul Heyer (New York: Longman, 1999) 288–300.

for forty years? The choice of the written word produced a mobile god without the weight of a two-ton golden calf.

With the coming of the printing press, Martin Luther called the invention the "supremist [sic] act of grace by which the Gospel can be driven forward."[2] According to Dickens, Luther's theses probably sold over 300,000 copies between 1517 and 1520.[3] Before the printing press, the clergy and monks were the "keepers" of the word, enabling the church to monopolize written communication. With the advent of the printing press, the translation of the Bible into vernacular allowed greater access to the "Word." As Aston says, "Printing was recognized as a new power... the printing presses transformed the field of communications and fathered an international revolt. It was a revolution."[4]

Like the Hebrews, the Protestants centered their attention on the "Word." Even today, Protestant evangelists on television pound their Bibles as they attest to the fact that "the Word is the way," and it can be found by reading the Bible. This method of communication could be contrasted with Catholicism, which chose more of the oral and visual traditions to communicate to and proselytize early Christians who were largely illiterate. Magnificent statues and paintings, commissioned by the Church, told the story of Christianity. Catholics are never told to read the Bible. Instead, believers listen to priests as they convey their interpretations of the Bible to the congregation, an example of an oral tradition that continues today throughout the world.[5]

Eisenstein, however, looked at how it took nearly 400 years from the time of Gutenberg's first Bible until the masses had access to mass-produced books.[6] The spread of a technology is often dependent on an

---

[2] *Ibid.*, 290.

[3] Arthur Geoffrey Dickens, *Reformation and Society in Sixteenth-Century Europe* (New York: Harcourt, Brace and World, 1966).

[4] Margaret Aston, *The Fifteenth Century: The Prospect of Europe* (New York: Harcourt, Brace and World, 1968) 76.

[5] Postman and Paglia, "Two Cultures," 293.

[6] Elizabeth Eisenstein, *The Printing Press as an Agent of Change: Communications and Cultural Transformations in Early Modern Europe* (New York: Cambridge University Press, 1980).

infrastructure along with social transformation. The mass produced book, as we know it today, is nothing like the Gutenberg Bible, which was produced to simulate the hand written manuscripts of the time and was only affordable by the elite. It required the hides of fifty sheep just to produce one book, a very expensive proposition, both in time and money. Paper, however, was not considerably cheaper to produce. Even in the mid-1800s, paper manufacturers in the United States found it to be cost-efficient to ship mummies from Egypt so that linen from the mummies could be processed into paper.

Lee tells us that the Fourdrinier process, introduced from Germany in 1867, allowed paper to be made from wood pulp. Before this new process, paper had been made by hand from rag stock. During the American Civil War, the cost of paper was $440 a ton. By 1899, however, a chemically produced wood pulp helped dramatically reduce the price to $42 a ton.[7] So, it was the affordability of paper, perhaps more than movable type, that affected the mass production of books, making them available to more people and thereby enabling the spread of literacy. In a similar observation on radio in Appalachia (see chapter 5), I found that it was perhaps the arrival of electricity into the region more than the medium itself that changed people's listening habits. Another reason for changing listening habits was the declining price of radio sets as mass production and competition between manufacturers occurred. Cheaper radio prices allowed more people to purchase sets and listen at home.

In *Technology and Ideology: The Case of the Telegraph*, Carey observed how the telegraph was the first technology that effectively separated communication from transportation. Before the telegraph, most non-interpersonal communication relied on the physical movement of messages (e.g. via foot messenger, horseback, or ship).[8] As communication technology has collapsed our previous notions of time

---

[7] Alfred McClung Lee, *The Daily Newspaper in America: The Evolution of a Social Instrument* (New York: The Macmillan Company, 1937).

[8] James Carey, "Technology and Ideology: The Case of the Telegraph," *Prospects* 8 (1983): 303–25. There were, however, pre-electric signaling devices such as semaphores that required an unobstructed line-of-sight.

and space, the time necessary for the movement of information has dramatically shrunk. This concept of spatialization calls attention to the importance of spatial distance as a hindrance to growth, but with communication technology, it is no longer as significant as it once was. Mosco observed that the ability to shrink the time it takes to move messages (along with goods and people) over space decreases the significance of spatial distance as a constraint.[9] Thus, it appears the Internet and electronic communications technology could especially benefit Appalachia, given the region's geographical isolation and mountainous terrain.

Stefik tells us that you cannot do anything by yourself on the Internet. It is about communicating within a community. When you go to a Web site, you are viewing the messages another has placed there.[10] Perhaps the popularity of AOL over smaller Internet service providers can be explained by the built-in communities one finds on AOL's proprietary sites. Like the library, with its bulletin boards and community interest groups, the Internet provides a virtual space where people can gather. At the end of the twentieth century, Apple's IMAC commercials had the perplexed actor Jeff Goldblum saying that if you do not have e-mail you cannot participate. Today, the Internet can bring people closer together. Someone using a conferencing software whiteboard in New York can virtually touch the digital paintbrush of a lover in California as they simultaneously doodle on an electronic screen. One must wonder at what Disney will do when all it takes to create a virtual environment is a closet with a screen and speakers. As with the cotton gin, which was partially responsible for the industrial revolution, the computer is bringing about a communications revolution.

In his routine, comedian Jackie Mason talks about how you might welcome a conversation with a stranger in a chat room who has just returned from climbing Mount Everest; however, if that same person knocked on your door and told you he had just returned from climbing

---

[9] Vincent Mosco, *The Political Economy of Communication: Rethinking and Renewal* (Thousand Oaks CA: Sage Publications, 1996).

[10] Mark Stefik, ed., *Internet Dreams: Archetypes, Myths, and Metaphors* (Cambridge: MIT Press, 1996).

the world's tallest peak, you would likely tell him to get off your porch. The Internet has allowed strangers to interact with one another. Although an Internet user may be alone in his or her home while chatting with a stranger in a chat room, some participants I spoke with compared their early experiences on the Internet with "the good ol' days" when one sat on the front porch and made small talk with the occasional passerby. In fact, what this brings to mind is what might be called "the Internet as electronic front porch."

It is therefore important to be mindful of how mutually influencing technologies and social and economic transformation affect the dissemination of most communication technologies.

Media in Appalachia

Historically, the development of rural areas has occurred where natural resources or land can be exploited. In his seminal piece, "After Bicycles, What?" Smythe described his 1972 conversation with the vice-chairman of the Chinese Communist Party. Viewing technology as being loaded with ideology, Smythe observed that when the Communists came to power in China, there was no north-south railroad. The railroad had been designed to serve the interests of those who wanted to exploit China's natural resources. The rail system was not built to serve the interests of the people of China; it was designed to ship natural resources to ports along the eastern coast.[11] Upon viewing Appalachia's history, one might see similarities; outsiders first appropriated land and then its natural resources.

Today, new development in a region depends largely on a telecommunications infrastructure and human resources. With sophisticated telecommunications, spatialization issues such as traversing mountainous terrain or great distances to a major hub (as within a good deal of Appalachia) have become less important. Melody observed that many could benefit from the growth of the communication sector, but those without an upgraded digital telephone system, such as ISDN, would be

---

[11] Dallas Walker Smythe, "After Bicycles, What?" in *Counterclockwise: Perspectives on Communication*, ed. Thomas Guback (Boulder: Westview Press, 1994) 230–44.

left out, specifically when speaking of sophisticated Internet access.[12] This "digital divide" is especially noticeable within rural areas of Appalachia. The National Telecommunications and Information Administration (NTIA) report "Falling through the Net" found that "rural areas are less likely to be connected [to the Internet] than urban areas. Regardless of income level, those living in rural areas are lagging behind in computer and Internet access. At some income levels, those in urban areas are fifty percent more likely to have Internet access than those earning the same income in rural areas."[13]

Other disparities between information "haves" and "have-nots," as cited in the above report, were lower education levels, lower income levels, and minority race status. These issues seem especially important when examining Internet usage in the Melungeon community.

Parker and Hudson have championed telecommunications technology as an aid to the development of rural areas like Appalachia because, as in urban areas, most new rural jobs will be in the service sector. Airline reservation centers have realized that centers using telecommunications technology can be set up in Caribbean nations more economically than in the United States. Two factors they found appealing were: (1) labor costs are cheaper in developing nations and (2) governments are often very accommodating in assisting international businesses with technological needs. Arguments have been made for a stronger public policy formation that would establish a new Marshall Plan for depressed areas in this country, specifically through telecommunications development. In the past, regulatory policies have contributed to a more equal distribution of new communication.[14]

---

[12] William Melody, "On the Political Economy of Communication in the Information Society," in *Illuminating the Blindspots: Essays Honoring Dallas W. Symthe*, ed. Dallas Smythe, Janet Wasko, Vincent Mosco, and Manjunath Pendakur (Norwood NJ: Ablex Pub. Corp., 1993) 63–81.

[13] National Telecommunications & Information Administration, "Falling Through the Net: New Commerce Report Shows Dramatic Growth in Number of Americans Connected to Internet." http://www.ntia.doc.gov/ntiahome/press/fttn070899.htm. Accessed 12 November 2006.

[14] Edwin B. Parker and Heather E. Hudson, *Electronic Byways: State Policies for Rural Development through Telecommunications* (Boulder: Westview Press, 1992).

According to Melody, the same telephone technology that was installed in urban areas was also installed in rural areas, partly because regulatory policies dictated that part of the profits from long distance services should be used for rural installations.[15] Mosco and Rideout view the recent United States governmental move towards regulatory liberalization (the aim of which is to increase market competition) as partially responsible for the removal of universality in telephony as private companies are freed to pursue their own market interests. With limited government intervention, rural areas of the nation currently without telephone systems able to handle digital data transfers are specifically at a disadvantage.[16]

However, there are caveats to heed as we examine the "development" of Appalachia. As Smythe points out, no technology is politically neutral. Technology has in the past disguised imperialist policies, and today it can be seen as the opiate of the educated public.[17] As Parker and Hudson point out, many rural residents do not necessarily want a handout as much as an equal opportunity.[18] This was certainly my feeling when speaking to Appalachian participants in this study. These attitudes are an example of the kind of social/political/economic context necessary for fully understanding the history of media outside of mere technological innovation.

---

[15] Melody, "On the Political Economy of Communication," 68-73.

[16] Vincent Mosco and Vanda Rideout, "Media Policy in North America," in *International Media Research: A Critical Survey*, ed. John Corner, Philip Schlesinger, and Roger Silverstone (London: Routledge, 1997) 154-83.

[17] Smythe, "After Bicycles, What?" 230-44.

[18] Parker and Hudson. *Electronic Byways*, 37-40.

Chapter Two

Uncovering Oral History

The Importance of Memory

There is a parlor game in which players are asked, "If given the chance to live your fantasy for a year, would you choose to do so if it meant not being able to recall the experience once it ended?" The question raises many issues. Loftus tells us that "without memory, life would consist of momentary experiences that have little relation to one another.... Memory is central to being human; thus it will come as no surprise that philosophers and scientists have been interested in the subject as far back as recorded history goes."[1] From an oral history perspective, the person whose memory is being examined is as important as the memory itself. Thompson points to the fact that until recently the lives of ordinary people were given little attention by historians, who have traditionally focused their attention on social and political leaders.[2] But examining the past from the point of view of the unprivileged perhaps provides us with a fairer reconstruction of history, thereby allowing history to become more democratic. As Ritchie puts it, "Generals in the rear may know the broad sweep of the battle plan, but foot soldiers will have a different view of the action on the battlefield; those at the center of events can proudly

---

[1] Elizabeth Loftus, "Tricked by Memory," in *Memory and History: Essays on Recalling and Interpreting Experience* (New York: University Press of America, 1994) 18.

[2] Paul Richard Thompson, *The Voice of the Past: Oral History* (Oxford: Oxford University Press, 1978).

recount their own accomplishments, but those on the periphery are often better able to make comparisons between the principal actors."[3] It seems unreasonable to rely on history written exclusively from the point of view of the governing elite, given their isolation from the lives of ordinary people. When George Herbert Walker Bush was president in the early 1990s, he and his entourage paid a visit to a supermarket where he made a small purchase. When the cashier swiped the item over the price scanner, the president was amazed by the technology, having never before seen a scanner in a grocery store. The power of oral history lies in the words and feelings of the foot soldiers, the people who go to the grocery store every day. Given the oral traditions of rural Appalachia, I believe oral history interviews can best convey what impact electronic media technology had on Appalachian residents.

Larson[4] examined how the twentieth century witnessed an explosion of the "electronic word" in many forms, while Ong[5] looked at how this explosion of orally based media transformed our society in ways that resemble primitive oral cultures. Specifically, Ong observed that radio (along with other electronic technology) "brought us into an age of 'secondary orality.' This new orality has striking resemblances to the old in its participatory mystique, its fostering of a communal sense, and even its use of formulas."[6]

As Ritchie found, other new technology has certainly enhanced, if not ultimately made the work of the oral historian possible. The use of a tape recorder not only provides the historian the words of the participant, it can also give hints to the social status of the speaker via dialect and grammar, in addition to any nuances of humor or sarcasm.[7] However, issues of validity should also be addressed when looking at the

[3] Donald A. Ritchie, foreword to *Memory and History: Essays on Recalling and Interpreting Experience*, ed. Jaclyn Jeffrey and Glenace Edwall (New York: University Press of America, 1994) vi.

[4] Charles Larson, *Persuasion: Reception and Responsibility* (Belmont CA: Wadsworth, 1992).

[5] Walter Ong, *Orality and Literacy: The Technologizing of the Word* (London: Metheun, 1982).

[6] *Ibid.*, 136.

[7] Donald Ritchie, *Doing Oral History* (New York: Twayne Publishers, 1995).

use of recording devices in relationship to historical documents. For instance, Sontag examined the photographer's goal of "mirroring reality," yet she was also aware of the photographer's pressing issues of style. When one looks at a photograph of a farm family from the 1930s, do we really get a sense of how that family lived? Chances are, everyone donned their Sunday finest for the picture.[8] Even with film, audio, and videotape, do we get a true representation of the event being recorded? The historian must recognize the consequences of the "Hawthorne Effect," which states that merely studying a group changes the outcome.[9]

The psychological state of an informant also affects memory. For example, members of a radical 1960s group might be reluctant to describe acts of sabotage in which they may have participated. Maybe they've become conservative businesspeople and radically changed their political perspective or simply may not wish to incriminate themselves. This does not mean they no longer recall certain events. The fact that they hide information may say more than the information they are hiding. In parsing out nuggets of truth, the oral historian must sometimes distinguish among folktales, anecdotes, and legends. By familiarizing oneself with the folktales within the region being studied, one is better equipped to recognize a tale being told, determine how it may differ from the "basic" tale, and discern what social processes might have contributed to the changes. It is incumbent upon social historians to rethink oppositional terms such as "insider/outsider" and "scholars/activists." The ideal of "apprehend[ing] and inscrib[ing] others in such a way as not to deny or diffuse their claims to subjecthood" should be the goal of all social scientists.[10]

Conducting oral history interviews is fraught with challenges, particularly when the interviewer is viewed as an outsider by the interviewees. In this study, some participants, uncomfortable with an interviewer entering into a region where many are burdened by low

---

[8] Susan Sontag, *On Photography* (New York: Farrar, Straus and Giroux, 1977).

[9] Richard Gillespie, *Manufacturing Knowledge: A History of the Hawthorne Experiments* (New York: Cambridge University Press, 1991).

[10] Frances Mascia-Lees, "The Postmodernist Turn in Anthropology: Cautions from a Feminist Perspective" *Signs* 15/1 (Autumn 1989): 12.

education levels, were reluctant to be recorded. Given the way the media often depict Appalachians in movies (*Deliverance*), television (*The Beverly Hillbillies*), and comic strips (*Snuffy Smith*), their reluctance is not surprising. I was always mindful of this fact and constantly struggled with how to mediate between the participants' discomfort and my responsibilities as an oral historian. I believe that my ability to identify with some of the participants' feelings (as I struggled with my own "outsider" feelings) assisted me in finding interviewees who were willing to share their stories and express themselves in their own words.

During my initial interviews about radio, I required a group old enough to recall the inception of this new medium into this region of the country. As a result, I actively sought elderly residents for discussions in community centers, nursing homes, retirement communities, and senior citizen centers. After meeting with the first group, a snowball effect occurred where participants suggested individuals and social clubs they felt might be interested in participating in the discussion. In addition to interviewing Appalachians at community and retirement centers, I began to be invited into some interviewees' private homes. This broadened the age group of the participants in the study from twenty-two years of age to 103. Three interviews were conducted by telephone, and some occurred at neighborhood potluck dinner parties. Occasionally, I would bump into some of the interviewees at community events such as dances and conferences or while shopping. These casual meetings often led to introductions to other members of the community interested in sharing stories about electronic media usage in rural Appalachia. As I extended my research agenda into examining television and the Internet's impact on the region, the snowball effect became more important to my sample pool. One interview in Sneedville, Tennessee, took place in the backroom of a barbershop where I interviewed the barber (who was a former county judge), the current judge, and other citizens of the town. I also began attending annual meetings of the Melungeon Heritage Association where I interviewed attendees about their electronic media usage and its impact on Melungeon identity.

Throughout my travels in Appalachia, I had the opportunity to interview a 103-year-old woman, the only African American in one town in Virginia (who had no trouble remembering her first ride in a Model-T Ford but unfortunately had no recollection of the arrival of radio in the region), and a minister who invited me to stay at his church's retreat whenever I was in the area doing research. Depending on the age of the participants, the period we discussed was from 1920 to the present day. In total, eighty-six oral history interviews were conducted, each lasting from twenty minutes to more than two hours. (See Appendix A for a complete list of each participant, his or her birthplace, and year of birth.)

The initial interviews at the various community centers included all members who attended. Groups over four and as large as nine necessitated the use of videotape as the primary recording tool. The videos proved invaluable in identifying speakers in the transcription process, especially when more than one participant spoke at once. Before starting my recorder, I would ask interviewees to sit in a semi-circle facing the camera. The use of a story-circle, whereby each question was posed and participants responded in order, helped trigger memories of other interviewees in the group. This proved particularly helpful with elderly participants. The original concept for the story circle has been described as a metaphor for the Native American Circle of Life. For example, Bruchac described the story-circle as a process whereby each phase of life is represented in the interview procedure. The "child" represents phase one, where we listen to stories. The "adolescent" represents phase two, where we observe the context of a story. The "adult" represents the third stage, where we recall stories from our youth, and lastly, the "elder" represents phase four, where stories we have learned are shared with others.[11] Banks calls attention to the impact of the four phases upon the interviewer in an oral history setting. He argues that phase one represents the collection of data by the interviewer; in phase two, the interviewer places data into various contextual frames; in phase three, the interviewer compares current data with other data from a similar period; in phase four, the interviewer shares compiled information with an audience.[12]

---

[11] Joseph Bruchac *Lasting Echoes: An Oral History of Native American People* (San Diego: Harcourt Brace and Co, 1997).

[12] Dennis Banks, "The Impact of Oral History on the Interviewer: A Study of

As with much qualitative research today, the interrelationship between the interviewer and the interviewee is of great importance. However, within story-circle group dynamics, the interrelationship amongst the interviewees is of equal importance. For example, with subsequent interviews where a large number of participants were available, I asked interviewees to break up into smaller groups for recording. This seemed to defuse the anxiety of some who watched the first group being interviewed. Once comfortable with the topic, many onlookers were eager to join the second group being recorded. Others remained off-camera but would interject comments or suggest words for a stumbling friend. When invited into the group by myself or other interviewees, most onlookers chose to remain on the sidelines. As mentioned above, this could have been for many reasons: fear of speaking on camera, fear of speaking in front of others, concern for not appearing "smart enough," or simply feeling their stories were of little interest to others. Although I would try to enlist participation from each person attending these meetings, I made it very clear that no one would be pressured to join the conversation if he or she chose simply to observe.

In addition to the formal, structured interview sessions, either in story-circle groups or individually, there were many times when I was without my recorder and simply had casual, often spontaneous conversations with members of the community. After these unrecorded conversations, I would try to jot down notes in a small notebook when I was alone. Lindlof tells of how some researchers in these situations record their notes during frequent visits to the restroom.[13] During my unstructured conversations, new questions came to mind that I would later use during structured/recorded interview sessions. More importantly, perhaps, these conversations gave me a truer insight into the lives of the people about whom I would be writing.

Novice Historians" (paper presented at the annual meeting of the National Council for the Social Studies, Cincinnati, OH, 20–23 November 1997).

[13] Thomas R. Lindlof, *Qualitative Communication Research Methods* (Thousand Oaks CA: Sage Publications, 1995).

I always tried to keep in mind Shaffir and Stebbins's idea that field workers should experience the culture they are examining through the eyes of the members they are studying.[14] However, this would sometimes become more complex than I would have imagined. For example, one interviewee, as stated above, was a minister in Sneedville, Tennessee, who invited me to stay at his congregation's retreat. This invitation allowed me to become more than just an outside observer by giving me the opportunity to live and eat with the people I was interviewing. By no means did I become a member of the community, but while attending church services the first Sunday night, the minister (who was always telling tall tales) introduced me to the congregation as the long lost grandson (who incidentally was a fugitive from the law) of a recently departed member of the community. Before I could extricate myself from this yarn, an elderly gentleman came up to me, saying that he wanted to shake my hand because "my grandfather" had saved his life. It was difficult to get the man to believe that the minister was just kidding, as the man continued to insist that I looked just like my grandfather.

Traveling around Appalachia, I would stop to interview someone in his or her home, and most often, I would be obliged to stay for supper. Yet even though I was surprisingly successful in finding participants eager to share their stories, I was also mindful of the fact that I was, to many, a stranger with a recorder. When people gave me the name of someone to interview, they often simply told me "go over to his or her house, knock on the door, and introduce yourself." However, I was always a little reluctant to pursue anyone without an introduction. Once, when I arrived unannounced at a man's business, his sons told me that their father was at home, and they gladly gave me directions. Driving up to the gentleman's house, I recognized his car coming toward me and turned mine around to give chase. As we passed his place of business, his sons enthusiastically waved me on. I finally caught up with him in town. After introducing myself, the man excused himself, saying that he was too busy to speak to me and went into Hardee's for lunch. Some people had no interest in a stranger with a tape recorder.

---

[14] William Shaffir and Robert A. Stebbins, eds. *Experiencing Fieldwork: An Inside View of Qualitative Research* (Newbury Park: Sage Publications, 1991).

There are, however, some advantages to being viewed as an outsider. For example, Thompson,[15] Guy,[16] and Yow[17] all address the sometime benefits of being an outsider when recording oral history, not the least of which being the ability to view the situation from a neutral perspective. As Thompson states, "The outsider can ask for the obvious to be explained; while the insider, who may in fact be misinformed in assuming the answer, does not ask for fear of seeming foolish."[18] Of course, I was constantly balancing on the fine line between asking simple questions with the intent of getting the participant to open up and asking questions that might be seen as simply ignorant.

Certainly, interpretive researchers have been criticized for attempting to speak "for" a group of people. One must ever be sensitive to issues of power, class, identity, gender, and race. Research should be approached as a discourse: a coordinated process of socially-constructed meaning.[19] As an example of my approach to research as socially constructed discourse, I noticed that on some occasions, when I first began recording oral histories in Appalachia, participants, especially elderly Appalachians, would get caught up in telling tales from the past. Having always loved stories, I can only assume that the pleased expression on my face must have encouraged the storytellers.[20] Although I would try my best to allow the interviewee to go in any direction the story would take him or her, some participants' stories about early radio

---

[15] Thompson, *The Voice of the Past*, 117.

[16] Roger Guy, "Down Home: Perception and Reality among Southern White Migrants in Post World War II Chicago," *The Oral History Review* 24/2 (December 1997): 35–52.

[17] Valerie Yow, "Do I Like Them Too Much?: Effects of the Oral History Interview on the Interviewer and Vice-Versa," *The Oral History Review* 24/1 (Summer 1997): 55–79.

[18] Thompson, *The Voice of the Past*, 117.

[19] Stephen, A. Tyler, "Post-Modern Ethnography: From Document of the Occult to Occult Document" in *Writing Culture: The Poetics and Politics of Ethnography*, ed. James Clifford and George E. Marcus (Berkeley: University of California Press, 1986) 122–40.

[20] Of course, I was also aware of a potential negative effect of this social construction. One must be sensitive to the possibility that participants might tailor their stories to get a positive reaction from the interviewer.

triggered my own memories of early television and its impact on my life. I often found myself telling stories about my own early memories of television. This give and take, I believe, helped put the participant at ease and facilitated the flow of information.

Interviews and Analysis

Lindlof says, "Interviews are especially well suited to helping the researcher understand a social actor's own perspective."[21] Although my spontaneous interviews helped gain the trust of many participants, I attempted to structure my formal interviews, where I used a tape or video recorder, in as relaxed a manner as possible. I would often chat casually with the participants before turning on the recorder. When I sensed that the interviewee was beginning to settle down, I would announce that I was about to start recording. After recording, I would again make casual conversation for another minute or two. I also paid careful attention to microphone placement. I would try not to place the mic in the sight line between the participant and myself. This helped insure that the interviewee would be looking at me and not the microphone when he or she spoke. Often, this allowed the participant to forget that his or her words were being recorded and made for a more relaxed interview.

After completing the interviews, I began "living with the data."[22] I listened to (or watched) the tapes and read the transcripts and my notes repeatedly until I began to recognize patterns. Often, while rereading the transcripts, images of the participants would appear in my mind's eye. While listening to or watching tapes, I paid careful attention to voice inflections. The way a speaker's voice became excited at a certain point or softer at another added insight into the person's feelings on the topic being discussed. To take account of these tone/tempo variations, I would make parenthetical notes in the transcript. If, for example, a

---

[21] Lindlof, *Qualitative Communication Research Methods*, 167.

[22] Jenny Nelson, "Phenomenology as Feminist Methodology: Explicating Interviews, in *Doing Research on Women's Communication: Perspectives on Theory and Method*, ed. Kathryn Carter and Carole Spitzack (Norwood NJ: Ablex Pub. Corp., 1989) 221–41.

person giggled while speaking, I would simply write "[giggle]" before his or her statement.

The recollections of many of the participants I interviewed were so rich that I feel fortunate to have been able to record them and am eager to share them. I attempted to keep quotes as close to the original as possible. Some oral history purists feel that the transcription of the recorded interview is sacrosanct. Many feel that editing out pauses distorts the participant's message. Others feel that such a concession is a small price to pay for easier readability. I did remove some "uhs," to facilitate the flow of the statements unless they contributed to the feeling or meaning of the quote.

I also felt it imperative to maintain the vernacular of the region whenever it occurred. A statement like "I've been a-knowin' these people since childhood" conveys feelings of ongoing familiarity (continuing from past into present and perhaps into the future), which is not quite as well conveyed in the more standardized "I've known these people since childhood." The use of the vernacular should be seen as contributing to the interpretation of the participant's feelings and "informed by the unique context in which they live."[23]

As in most oral histories, I use the participants' names since I do not want those who were interviewed to feel that I am speaking for them or taking away their voice. However, the analysis and interpretations are mine. Given that I was on a first-name basis with most of the people I interviewed, after using a participant's full name the first time I refer to them, I use only their given name on subsequent references or citations.

Throughout the interview process, I tried not to rely too heavily on my prepared questions and allowed the interviewee to follow any unexpected path he or she chose to take. Of course, my initial questions did shape the direction in which I felt I could derive the most raw material (memories), and I tried my best to guide participants in the direction that best served my scholarly aim. As the author of this work, I also recognize that I chose the quotes that are included herein (see

[23] Paul Rabinow, *Reflections on Fieldwork in Morocco* (Berkeley: University of California Press, 1977) 103.

Appendix B for a list of questions used during my oral history interviewing process).

In *A Shared Authority*, Frisch addresses the notion that the interviewer may feel more responsible for the creation of a work; however, the interviewee is the greater partner. It is in the interviewee's stories that the greatest value of an oral history resides. Furthermore, the interviewee also participates in the interpretation of the stories since he or she constantly analyzes their own motives while recalling them.[24] "Critical ethnographers," writes Stacey, "eschew a detached stance of neutral observation, and they perceive their subjects as collaborators in a project the researcher can never fully control. Moreover, they acknowledge the indispensably intrusive and unequal nature of their participation in the studied culture."[25] I have always felt that telling one's story can be cathartic and hope that participants in this study benefited from telling their stories.

---

[24] Michael Frisch, *A Shared Authority: Essays on the Craft and Meaning of Oral and Public History* (Albany: State University of New York Press, 1990). Also see Ritchie, *Doing Oral History*, 111-19.

[25] Judith Stacey, "Can There Be a Feminist Ethnography?" in *Women's Words: The Feminist Practice of Oral History*, ed. Sherna Berger Gluck and Daphne Patai (New York: Routledge, 1991) 115.

Chapter Three

Appalachia on My Mind[1]: Outsiders' Construction of Appalachian Identity

"Squeal like a pig!"[2]

This line from the motion picture *Deliverance* conjures up as much unadulterated fear, disgust, and horror as almost any other line in motion picture history. Just as *Jaws* kept a generation out of the ocean, *Deliverance* kept it from vacationing in the Appalachians. Appalachia remains the last refuge where, in this politically correct society, with a quick aside, it is still acceptable to target its residents with racial slurs. "In six months" observed filmmaker John Waters, "no one will say 'white trash'...it's the last racist thing you can say and get away with."[3] That was over a decade ago.

Appalachia is many things to many people. Novelist Jesse Stuart said, "Appalachia is anywhere there's coal under the ground."[4] Perhaps one should start by defining Appalachia in geo-political terms. In 1965,

---

[1] Borrowed from Henry Shapiro's *Appalachia on Our Mind: The Southern Mountains and Mountaineers in the American Consciousness, 1870–1920* (Chapel Hill: The University of North Carolina Press, 1978).

[2] *Deliverance*, DVD, directed by John Boorman (1972; Burbank CA: Warner Home Video, 2004).

[3] Tad Friend, "White Hot Trash," *New York Magazine*, 22 August 1994, 23.

[4] Betty Garrett, "An Appalachian Author Describes His Life Style," *Appalachia* 6/3 (December 1972–January 1973): 24–28.

the Appalachian Regional Commission (ARC) simply defined the Appalachian region as consisting of 360 counties in eleven states from Alabama to Pennsylvania. Two years later, it changed its mind. In 1967, the ARC broadened its definition of Appalachia to include 397 counties and thirteen states ranging from as far north and east as New York to as far south and west as Mississippi. In 1990, an additional county was added along with yet another in 1991, bringing the total to 399 counties. In 1998, seven counties were added for a total of 406. In 2002, four more counties were added for a grand total of 410 counties comprising the Appalachian Region of the United States (see map 1).[5] In 2005, the US House of Representatives approved a bill that would add an additional twelve counties to the Appalachian Region.[6] Given the broad geographical region of Appalachia (approximately 6 percent of the country lies within the ARC boundaries), pinning down the term has always been problematic. Within the region, there are plateaus, ridges, valleys, piedmonts, several mountain ranges (see map 2), tiny "hollers," and major metropolitan areas. There are also poverty, welfare programs, geographical isolation, coal mines, and a multitude of complex cultures.

---

[5] *Encyclopedia of Appalachia* (Knoxville: University of Tennessee Press, 2006) s.v. Introduction.

[6] "Newsroom: Legislative Update," Appalachian Regional Commission, http://www.arc.gov/index.do?nodeId=39 (accessed 24 May 2006).

Map 1: Appalachian Counties

Appalachian Regional Commission

Map 2: Appalachian Topography

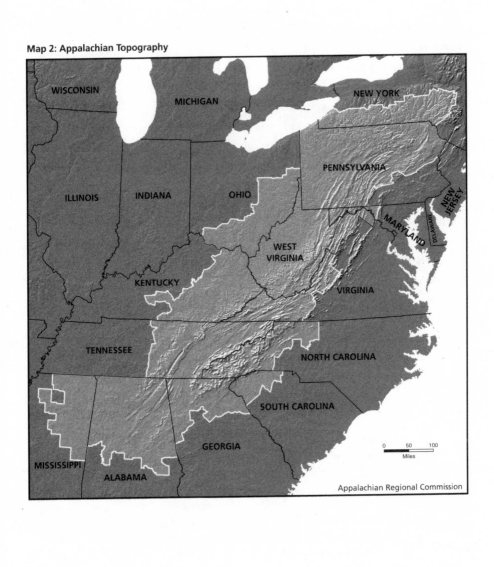

WISCONSIN

MICHIGAN

NEW YORK

PENNSYLVANIA

NEW JERSEY

ILLINOIS

INDIANA

OHIO

MARYLAND

DELAWARE

WEST VIRGINIA

KENTUCKY

VIRGINIA

TENNESSEE

NORTH CAROLINA

SOUTH CAROLINA

GEORGIA

MISSISSIPPI

ALABAMA

0   50   100
Miles

Appalachian Regional Commission

Some speculate that Appalachia was named by sixteenth-century Spanish explorers who took the name from the Apalachee Indian tribe of northern Florida. The term Appalachia was used from that time until the end of the nineteen century simply to denote the mountain system.[7] Euroamericans began settling in the region in the eighteenth century. As Salstrom found, "Between 1714 and 1775...thousands of rent-racked flax and linen producers abandoned their tiny leaseholds in Northern Ireland and flooded across the Atlantic to America, where many or most of them lit out for the territories of that day."[8] By 1790 approximately 250,000 Scotch-Irish[9] had settled in America, at least three-fourths of them within Appalachia.[10] In addition, thousands of Germans and immigrants from other European countries settled in the area. Although many landed in New York, the majority of these transatlantic immigrants arrived in Philadelphia. Later arrivals were directed to the ports of Wilmington and Charleston. Given that coastal areas were comparatively well-developed and land further west was considerably cheaper, many immigrants chose to settle inland. The diagonal flow patterns of the region's river system (e.g. the Roanoke and James) also facilitated the movement of these settlers (see map 3). As reason would dictate, early settlers chose the more fertile land adjacent to the Great Valley, and only later did they move further inland where the soil was of lesser quality, the slopes steeper, and the area more isolated.[11]

[7] Karl Raitz and Richard Ulack, "Regional Definitions," in *Appalachia: Social Context Past and Present*, ed. Bruce Ergood and Bruce Kuhre (Dubuque: Kendall/Hunt Publishing Company, 1991) 10–25.

[8] Paul Salstrom, *Appalachia's Path to Dependency: Rethinking a Region's Economic History, 1730–1940* (Lexington: University Press of Kentucky, 1994).

[9] Even though "Scot," meaning Scotsman, suggests the use of the term "Scots-Irish," the literature almost uniformly uses the term "Scotch-Irish," as will I throughout this work.

[10] Kenneth Keller, "What Is Distinctive about the Scotch-Irish?" in *Appalachian Frontiers: Settlement, Society, & Development in the Preindustrial Era*, ed. Robert Mitchell (Lexington: University Press of Kentucky, 1991) 69–86.

[11] John. B. Rehder, "The Scotch-Irish and English in Appalachia," in *To Build in a New Land: Ethnic Landscapes in North America*, ed. Allen Noble (Baltimore: The Johns Hopkins University Press, 1992) 95–118.

Map 3: Appalachian Topography with Rivers

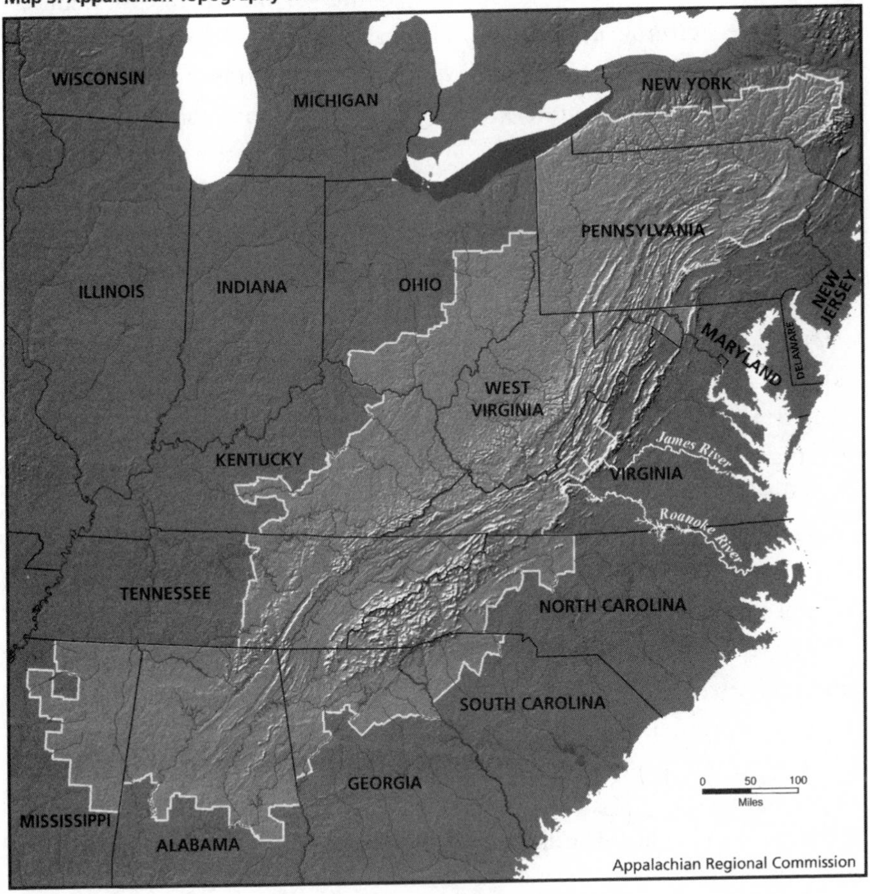

WISCONSIN

MICHIGAN

NEW YORK

PENNSYLVANIA

ILLINOIS

INDIANA

OHIO

NEW JERSEY

DELAWARE

MARYLAND

WEST VIRGINIA

KENTUCKY

James River

VIRGINIA

Roanoke River

TENNESSEE

NORTH CAROLINA

SOUTH CAROLINA

0   50   100
Miles

GEORGIA

MISSISSIPPI

ALABAMA

Appalachian Regional Commission

In the latter nineteenth century, the rest of the nation began to rediscover Appalachia and its setters. In 1895, William Goodell Frost, in a speech as president of Berea College,[12] first coined the phrase "Appalachian American," attributing to the region and its residents a distinctive cultural, economic, and social identity.[13] Batteau describes Appalachia as being a creature of the urban imagination, made up of folk culture, romantic fiction, journalism, and public policy.[14] Shapiro attributes much of Appalachia's "discovery" to the local-color movement during the period,[15] when writers such as John Fox, Jr. wrote stories about Kentucky mountain life in his novels such as *The Trail of the Lonesome Pine*[16] and *The Kentuckians*.[17] According to Shapiro, between 1870 and 1890, new magazines such as *Lippincott's*, *Scribner's*, and *Harper's New Monthly Magazine* brought stories that explored little-known aspects of Appalachian life to much of genteel, middle-class America.[18] Will Wallace Harney's travel piece for *Lippincott's*, titled "A Strange Land and Peculiar People," dealt with his journey to the Cumberland Mountains in 1869, although little in the article seemed to warrant such an off-putting title.[19] Another writer, Will Allen Dromgoole, wrote of her travel experiences in the mountains of Tennessee where she encountered a group called the Malungeons.[20] Her 1891 article, "The Malungeon Tree and Its Four Branches," published in *The Arena* magazine, unflatteringly described these mountain

---

[12] Located in Berea, Kentucky, Berea College was a co-educational institution enrolling African American and white students from 1870 until 1904, when segregation was mandated by the Kentucky legislature.

[13] Shapiro, *Appalachia on Our Mind*, 68.

[14] Allen Batteau, *The Invention of Appalachia* (Tucson: Arizona Press, 1990).

[15] Shapiro, *Appalachia on Our Mind*, 3-31.

[16] John Fox, Jr., *The Trail of the Lonesome Pine* (New York: Harper & Brothers Publishers, 1898).

[17] John Fox, Jr., *The Kentuckians* (New York: C. Scribner's Sons, 1908).

[18] Shapiro, *Appalachia on Our Mind*, 6.

[19] Will Wallace Harney, "A Strange Land and Peculiar People," *Lippincott's Magazine* 12/31 (October 1873) 429-38, as cited in Shapiro, *Appalachia on Our Mind*, 115-116.

[20] Although "Melungeon" is the accepted current spelling, to remain faithful to cited text, other spellings will be found throughout this body of work.

residents and is still pointed to as an example of racial prejudice.[21] In addition, William Goodell Frost described the "mountainous backyards" of several eastern states in his 1899 *Atlantic Monthly* article titled "Our Contemporary Ancestors in the Southern Mountains."[22] In fact, between 1870 and 1890, more than 125 short stories were published relating to the nature of mountain life in this region of the country.[23]

Today, defining what makes up Appalachia continues to be elusive. As Whisnant observes, "Appalachia's boundaries have been drawn so many times by so many different hands that it is futile to look for a correct definition of the region."[24] For example, in looking at how students attending colleges and universities in Appalachia define the region, Ulack and Raitz found great discrepancies between the students' cognitive delineation of the area compared with the ARC's definition. Less than 20 percent of the students questioned believed that any part of New York fell within Appalachia and no one included Mississippi within the region. When asked to draw a boundary line enclosing what they perceived Appalachia to be, the majority of respondents (60 percent) included only one-third of the ARC region along the north-south axis and approximately one half of the east-west dimension. This region, according to the authors, "seems to be the most widely publicized as having the full range of negative Appalachian-associated characteristics: coal mining, flooding, environmental degradation, unemployment, poverty, and isolation."[25] In 1974, the ARC divided the region into northern, central, and southern subregions (see map 4). The central

---

[21] Will Allen Dromgoole, "The Malungeon Tree and Its Four Branches," *The Arena* 3 (June 1891): 470–79.

[22] William Goodell Frost, "Our Contemporary Ancestors in the Southern Mountains," *Atlantic Monthly* 83 (1899), as cited in Shapiro, *Appalachia on Our Mind*, 311-19.

[23] Carvel Collins, "Nineteenth Century Fiction of the Southern Appalachians," *Bulletin of Bibliography* 17 (1942): 186–90.

[24] David Whisnant, *Modernizing the Mountaineer: People, Power, and Planning in Appalachia* (New York: Burt Franklin, 1980) 134.

[25] Richard Ulack and Karl Raitz, "Appalachia: A Comparison of the Cognitive and Appalachian Regional Commission Regions," *Southeastern Geographer* 21/1 (May 1981): 52.

region,[26] characterized as the poorest, appeared to be the most widely recognized as representing Appalachia in the mental maps of the students participating in the Ulack and Raitz study.

A year before the ARC divided the region into three sections, Zelinsky identified a subregion of the United States that he called the Upland South, which "comprises the Southern Appalachians, the Upper Appalachian Piedmont, the Cumberland and other low interior plateaus."[27] Although upland refers to an area of land of high elevation, the term Upland South takes on a cultural meaning in addition to its physiographic significance. According to Zelinsky, these cultural areas are a "naively perceived segment of the time space continuum distinguished from others on the basis of genuine differences in cultural systems."[28]

For the sake of this study, I will be using the all-inclusive 2002 ARC definition (see map 1). However, this is but one politically—and bureaucratically—defined view of Appalachia. By traveling to different regions of Appalachia, I hope my interviews reflect the "differences in cultural systems." Most of the interviews in my study were conducted in areas straddling the central subregion of Appalachia. Discussions taking place in southeastern Ohio and southwestern West Virginia fall into the southern most section of the ARC's northern region, while interviews in southwestern Virginia and northeastern Tennessee straddle the central and southern subregions (see map 4).

The "Other" White

Although a large percentage of Appalachians are of Scotch-Irish and German descent, it is imperative that we recognize that the population of the region has been influenced by immigrants from nearly every European nation, many of whom came to work in the Appalachian coal mines. According to Lewis, nearly 10 percent of coal miners in West

---

[26] The central region consists of southern West Virginia, southwestern Virginia, eastern Kentucky, and northeastern Tennessee.

[27] Wilbur Zelinsky, *The Cultural Geography of the United States* (Englewood Cliffs: Prentice-Hall, 1973) 123.

[28] *Ibid.*, 112.

Map 4: Appalachian Subregions

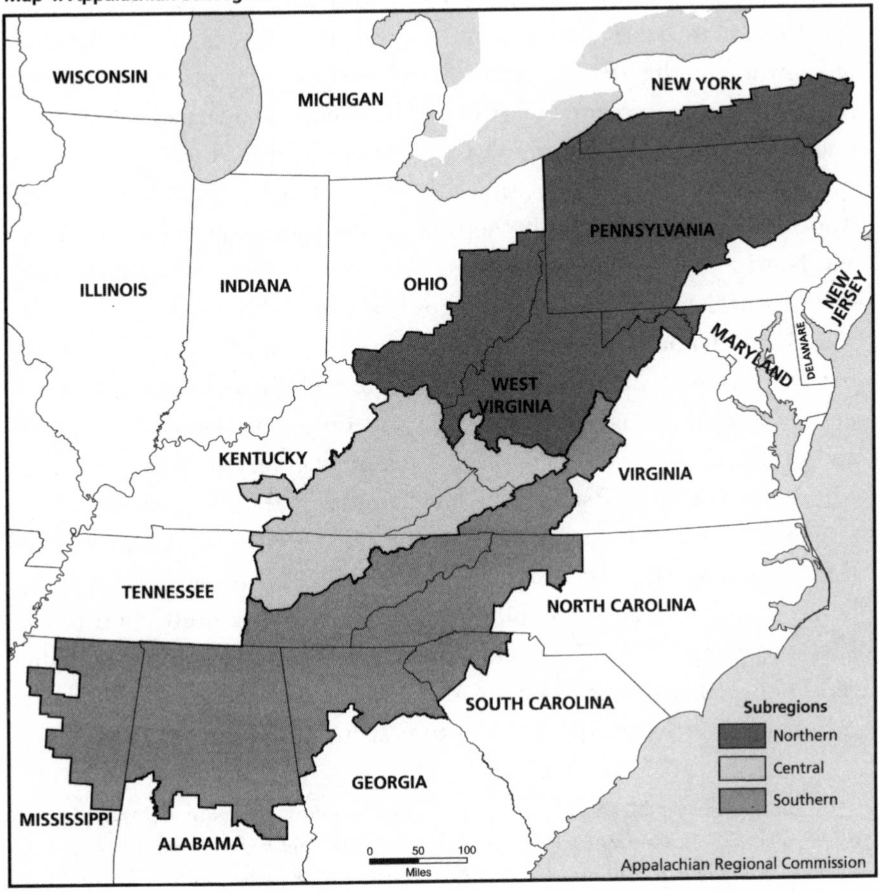

WISCONSIN

MICHIGAN

NEW YORK

PENNSYLVANIA

NEW JERSEY

ILLINOIS

INDIANA

OHIO

MARYLAND

DELAWARE

WEST VIRGINIA

KENTUCKY

VIRGINIA

TENNESSEE

NORTH CAROLINA

SOUTH CAROLINA

GEORGIA

MISSISSIPPI

ALABAMA

0   50   100
Miles

Subregions

Northern

Central

Southern

Appalachian Regional Commission

Virginia in 1909 were Italian and more than 5 percent were Hungarian. Poles, Slavs, and Russians each made up nearly 2 percent of the population. During the same period, more than 25 percent of coal miners listed by the West Virginia Department of Mines were African American, and nearly 18 percent of the total were listed as other or unknown.[29] In the 1970s, Nyden found that four out of five miners in the southwestern portion of Appalachian Pennsylvania had parents or grandparents who were born in eastern or southern Europe.[30]

However, for many, there is no ethnicity attached to the Appalachian other than white and, more specifically, poor white. Wray and Newitz describe "whiteness" as the norm, the "unrace" with the rest of the world falling into the category of the "other."[31] However, the stereotypical image of the mountain-dwelling Appalachian has often been projected by the media as a degenerate hillbilly, who arguably ranks below the other racist southern white stereotypes of "poor white trash" and "redneck." Appalachians have become segregated from "normal" whites not because of skin color but because of their supposedly more savage comportment. In essence, they are often seen as having arrived on the primitive side of our primitive/civilized binary. Williamson, however, argues that the hillbilly is no "other," but is a reflection of us. Like the village fool, we see him or her holding up a mirror, and the reflection is that of our worst fears, the image of ourselves.[32] To ignore the ethnic diversity of Appalachia is to perpetuate the stereotype.

[29] Ronald Lewis, "Beyond Isolation and Homogeneity: Diversity and the History of Appalachia," in *Confronting Appalachian Stereotypes: Back Talk from an American Region*, ed. Dwight B. Billings, Gurney Norman, and Katherine Ledford (Lexington: University Press of Kentucky, 1999) 21–46.

[30] Paul Nyden, *Black Coal Miners in the United States* (New York: The American Institute for Marxist Studies, 1974).

[31] Matt Wray and Annalee Newitz, *White Trash: Race and Class in America* (New York: Routledge, 1997).

[32] Jerry Wayne Williamson, *Hillbillyland: What the Movies Did to the Mountains and What the Mountains Did to the Movies* (Chapel Hill: University of North Carolina Press, 1995). For further discussion on the issue of identity and Appalachia, see Alan Banks, Dwight Billings, and Karen Tice, "Appalachian Studies and Postmodernism," in *Multicultural Experiences, Multicultural Theories*, ed. Mary Rogers et al. (New York: McGraw-Hill, 1996); Jane S. Becker, *Selling Tradition: Appalachia and the Construction*

Appalachian diversity is particularly evident in the group known as the Melungeons. Desiring a group old enough to recall the inception of radio and television, I actively sought elderly residents for discussions, the majority of whom were either of Scotch-Irish or German descent. However, few were Internet users. In searching for an indigenous group from within the Appalachian region who had actively embraced the Internet, I became aware of the Melungeon Heritage Association. This group began holding national conferences celebrating their tri-racial heritage in 1997.

Today, the largest Melungeon communities are primarily in eastern Tennessee, western North Carolina, and southwestern Virginia.[33] However, members are found throughout the Appalachian region and beyond. Perhaps some migrated in search of a place where their heritage was not suspect. Others may have been seeking employment in the city and are now living in diaspora. As Melungeons begin to reach out to embrace their heritage, many are using the Internet to trace their genealogy. Darlene Wilson, founder of one of the original Melungeon Web sites, claimed that a large percentage of the people who visit her Web site are expatriates from the communities of Appalachia.[34] Now,

---

of an American Folk, 1930–1940 (Chapel Hill: University of North Carolina Press, 1998); Chad Berry, Southern Migrants, Northern Exiles (Champaign: University of Illinois Press, 2000); Dwight Billings, Gurney Norman and Katherine Ledford, eds., Confronting Appalachian Stereotypes: Back Talk from an American Region (Lexington: University Press of Kentucky, 1999); Rodger Cunningham, "Scotch-Irish and Others," Appalachian Journal 18/1 (Fall 1990): 84-90; Rodger Cunningham, Apples on the Flood: The Southern Mountain Experience (Knoxville: University of Tennessee Press, 1987); Bruce Ergood and Bruce E. Kuhre, eds., Appalachia: Social Context Past and Present, 3rd ed. (Dubuque IA: Kendall/Hunt Publishing Company, 1991); Larry J. Griffin and Ashley B. Thompson, "Appalachia and the South: Collective Memory, Identity, and Representation," Appalachian Journal 29/3 (Spring 2002): 296–327; James Klotter, "The Black South and White Appalachia," Journal of American History 66/4 (March 1980): 832-849; Shapiro, Appalachia on Our Mind; Bob Snyder, "Image and Identity in Appalachia," Appalachian Journal 9/2 (1982): 124-133.

[33] See Brent Kennedy and Robyn Vaughan Kennedy, The Melungeons: The Resurrection of a Proud People: An Untold Story of Ethnic Cleansing in America (Macon GA: Mercer University Press, 1997).

[34] Darlene Wilson, interview with author, audio recording, 18 June 2004, in possession of author.

through the use of the Internet, the Melungeon community is perhaps defined less as a geographic community than as an electronic virtual community.

In the past, Appalachian identity has been largely defined by outsiders. Today, Melungeons are beginning to define themselves by authoring their own Web sites.[35] This shift in insider/outsider constructs of identity will be further examined in the next chapter, "Melungeon Construction of Identity."

---

[35] For example, see http://www.melungeon.org.

Chapter Four

Melungeon Construction of Identity

While interviewing rural Appalachians about their electronic media usage, I found that few of the elderly participants who recalled the inception of radio and television were Internet users. In fact, for some, the mere mention of the Internet brought suspicious looks. Several felt they were too old to learn about something they viewed as "not very personal" or "too technical." "You hear so much bad about it," Margaret Tabler said of the Internet, "I don't want one. Kids are abusing it."[1] Even participants in their fifties were resistant. Virginia Miller argued: "It's for the younger generation. For our generation, I think this newfound stuff is just too far beyond us. I think we're really scared of it, just like the older generation was scared when telephones come out. They were scared to use the telephone right at first because I know my dad would very seldom touch the telephone if it would ring. You know, he'd have one of us answer it."[2]

When asked if anyone felt "scared" of other emerging electronic media such as radio or television, Marian Dees replied: "No, because I was young. I was ready for anything."[3] Henry Shaffer reflected: "Well with radio...then we was kids, and we didn't think of anything ahead.

---

[1] Margaret Tabler, interview with author, audio recording, 11 May 1998, in possession of author.

[2] Virginia Miller, interview with author, video recording, 19 June 1998, in possession of author.

[3] Marian Dees, interview with author, audio recording, 30 June 1998, in possession of author.

Now this Internet is sort of scary because there is so much that's going on you just wonder—everybody knows your business. And you transmit, well, all over the world, and well, it's sort of scary. It's something that we don't know anything about and afraid to find out, I guess."[4]

As I continued to search for a group within Appalachia that had embraced the Internet, I was introduced to the Melungeon Heritage Association. In 1997, the association held its first gathering called First Union. Second Union followed in 1998. In 1999, the Melungeon Heritage Association held a genealogical workshop, which I attended. Prior to the gathering, I placed a notice on the Melungeon Web site announcing that while at the conference, I would be doing face-to-face oral history interviews to discuss participants' radio, television, and Internet usage. I also relied on a snowball effect resulting from recommendations of friends and neighbors of those initially interviewed. This required trips to Sneedville, Tennessee, and Wise, Virginia (areas currently with large Melungeon communities), for further interviews.

Many of the participants I first interviewed became involved in the Internet because of their interest in genealogy. As they examined their possible Melungeon roots, many went to the Internet for further research. Today, the Internet is used by tens of thousands of people doing genealogical research. One major genealogy Web site, cyndislist.com, claims over 8,800 subscribers to its listserv, more than 70,000 visitors to the Web site each day, and more than 2,000,000 visitors each month.[5]

In May 2000, I attended Third Union in Wise, Virginia, where I again was listed on the program as someone who would be conducting oral history interviews. Most recently, I interviewed participants at the Association's Fifth Union in Kingsport, Tennessee, in May 2004 and at the Frankfort, Kentucky gathering in July 2005.

---

[4] Henry Shaffer, interview with author, video recording, 17 June 1998, in possession of author.

[5] Cyndislist, http://www.cyndislist.com. Also see www.rootsweb.com; www.ancestry.com; Terri Lamb, *E-genealogy: Finding Your Family Roots Online* (Indianapolis: Sams, 2000); Elizabeth Crowe, *Genealogy Online* (New York: McGraw-Hill, 2000).

Melungeons in Appalachia

In the past, Appalachia has been overlooked by some because of its perceived unglamorous homogeny—white people living in a rugged area of the country. As Whisnant informs us, "The WASP image of Appalachia is certainly the result of biased historiography. Appalachia is certainly no less WASPish than the rest of the country, but it is nevertheless very mixed ethnically."[6] If what Eller says is true, that "no other region of the United States today plays the role of the 'other America' quite so persistently as Appalachia,"[7] then within this marginalized society, the Melungeon community, historically outcast within an outcast society, is doubly marginalized.

According to Kennedy, the Melungeon community descends from Turks, Berbers, Jews, Portuguese, Spaniards, and others who arrived on the southeastern seaboard of North America during the period between 1492 and the founding of Jamestown in 1607.[8] Others have described the Melungeons as a people of Mediterranean descent who settled in the Appalachian Mountains as early as 1567.[9] Davis identified the Melungeons as "dark-skinned, reddish-brown complexioned people [who were] supposed to be of Moorish descent, neither Indian nor

---

[6] David Whisnant, "Ethnicity and the Recovery of Regional Identity in Appalachia: Thoughts upon Entering the Zone of Occult Instability," *Soundings* 56/1 (Spring 1973): 125.

[7] Eller, foreward to *Confronting Appalachian Stereotypes*, ix.

[8] Brent Kennedy and Robyn Vaughan Kennedy, *The Melungeons: The Resurrection of a Proud People: An Untold Story of Ethnic Cleansing in America* (Macon GA: Mercer University Press, 1997).

[9] See Melanie Lou Sovine, "The Mysterious Melungeons: A Critique of Mythical Image" (Ph.D. diss., University of Kentucky, 1982); Bonnie Ball, *The Melungeon: Notes on the Origin of a Race* (Johnson City TN: The Overmountain Press, 1992); Jean Patterson Bible, *Melungeons Yesterday and Today* (Jefferson City TN: Bible, 1975); Saundra Keyes Ivey, "Oral, Printed, and Popular Culture Traditions Related to the Melungeons of Hancock County, Tennessee" (Ph.D. diss., Indiana University, 1976); Mattie Ruth Johnson, *My Melungeon Heritage: A Story of Life on Newman's Ridge* (Johnson City TN: Overmountain Press, 1997).

Negro, but [who] had fine European features, and claimed to be Portuguese."[10]

McGlothlen estimates the genealogical breakdown of the Melungeons as a group to be "one percent Native American, nine percent African and ninety percent European."[11] It seems remarkable that an author could estimate the genealogical breakdown of a group of people with such speculation. In fact, many of the books published on the Melungeon community have not necessarily adhered to the strictest academic research methods and have been criticized in the literature for deficient scholarship. N. Brent Kennedy, author of *The Melungeons: The Resurrection of a Proud People* and founder of the Melungeon Research Committee, is perhaps recognized within the community as its primary authority. Kennedy's book, however, has been described as "remarkably egocentric...[as he is] not only its author but its centerpiece from whom all description and argumentation radiate."[12]

Today, sociologists and anthropologists have identified Melungeons as "tri-racial isolates."[13] Their "mixed blood" led to discrimination that kept many from claiming or celebrating their heritage. Through the years, the term has taken on a negative connotation. Referring to "an enigmatic people known as Melungeons," Berry, an Edinburgh-trained sociologist who taught at Ohio State University from 1940 to 1955, recounts an "unholy" Melungeon legend: "Someone is sure to tell you that long ago the Devil—usually referred to thereabouts as Old Horney—was driven from Hell by his domineering wife, and wandered for a time over the face of the earth. Eventually he came to the mountains of Tennessee, which so reminded him of his old haunts that

---

[10] Louise Davis, "The Mystery of the Melungeons," *Nashville Tennessean*, 22 September 1963, 16.

[11] Mike McGlothlen, *Melungeons and other Mestee Groups* (Gainesville FL: Mike McGlothlen, 1994) 7.

[12] David Henige, "Brent Kennedy's Melungeons," *Appalachian Journal* 25/3 (Spring 1998): 271.

[13] Brewton Berry, *Almost White* (New York: Macmillan, 1963). In this text, Berry lists other groups he finds similar to Melungeons: "Guineas," "Jackson Whites," "Croatans," "Lumbees," "WINs" (White-Indian-Negro), "Red Bones," and "Brass Ankles."

he decided to settle down. And so he took himself an Indian squaw wife—and the race of Melungeons came of that unholy union."[14]

Indeed, the origin of the very word "Melungeon" is shrouded in mystery. Perhaps the most widely accepted explanation refers to the French word "mélange," meaning mixture or mixing. In his memoirs, Tennessee jurist Judge Lewis Shepherd stated that "the term 'Melungeon' is an East Tennessee provincialism; it was coined by the people of that country to apply to these people and is derived from the French word, mélange, meaning a mixture or medley and has gotten into modern dictionaries."[15] Cambiaire examined how French traders and trappers:

> Must have given the name of Melangeons to the descendants of a few white men and Indians, who originated the strange race of people now lost among descendants of the first American pioneers. As Melangeons from the French word, mélanger, means, "mixed breed," and as these people have English names, and speak old-time English, they certainly have English ancestry.... They could not have invented this name, because they did not want it, and the few American settlers in Tennessee at the time did not know enough French to call these newcomers Melangeons. Either they brought this name with them after some Frenchmen gave it to them, or some Frenchmen who lived and trapped in the vicinity, gave it to them.[16]

Another suggestion is that the word is of Turkish derivation. The word "melun," meaning damned, and "jun," meaning soul, combine to form "melun-jun" or "damned soul," a phrase with which some

---

[14] *Ibid.*, 16.

[15] Lewis Shepherd, "What Do You Know About The Melungeons?" *Nashville Banner*, 3 August 1924, 88.

[16] Celestin Pierre Cambiaire, *Western Virginia Mountain Ballads, The Last Stand of American Pioneer Civilization* (London: The Mitre Press, 1935) 4–6.

Melungeons might sympathize.[17] A far more exotic term, "melungo," possibly from the African/Portuguese word meaning shipmate, supports the legend that African/Portuguese sailors jumped ship while approaching the southeastern seaboard of North America. They may have been escaping slaves or mutineers fleeing to the mountains to hide. Some support this version based on the fact that Melungeons can still be found on Tennessee and Virginia mountain ridges. In his well-received article "Melungeon History and Myth" in the *Appalachian Journal*, Everett points to suggestions that the Melungeon was descended from "marooned" Portuguese sailors, but he continues to say that "never has anyone demonstrated that any actual cultural or ethnic Iberian connections exist between the handful of 17th century Eastern Shore 'Portuguese'—or for that matter, Portuguese from anywhere else—and the late 18th, 19th and 20th century Melungeons of Southern Appalachia."[18] However, in her doctoral dissertation, Ivey addressed the "exotic traditions of exploration in North America by a variety of national and racial groups...[who] became linked with the Melungeons." The list included "Phoenicians and Romans, the Lost Tribes of Israel, Prince Madoc's band of explorers, the Portuguese, the Lost Colony of Roanoke, and others."[19]

Throughout my interviews, I became aware of how many participants adopted/adapted elements of these legends to create their own ethnic lineages. For example, participants often claimed some

---

[17] For further discussion, see Kennedy and Kennedy, *The Melungeons*; Bible, *Melungeons Yesterday and Today*; Ball, *The Melungeons*.

[18] C. S. Everett, "Melungeon History and Myth," *Appalachian Journal* 26/4 (Summer 1999): 372–73.

[19] Ivey, "Oral, Printed, and Popular Culture Traditions," 80. The embracing of mythology to come to terms with identity is found throughout Melungeon folklore. As Ivey points out, some legends trace the Melungeon back to the Lost Tribes of Israel. The finding of Hebrew-inscribed coins dating from 132–134 CE in Kentucky added some credibility to this belief, although the fact that they were not professionally excavated casts additional doubt on this theory. For further discussion, see Cyrus Gordon, *Before Columbus* (New York: Crown Publishers, 1971). For further discussion on Madoc, allegedly a Welsh explorer who landed on the southeastern part of North American in 1170, see Richard Deacon, *Madoc and the Discovery of America* (New York: George Braziller, 1966).

degree of Portuguese ancestry. When asked how his family ended up on the rocky mountain ridges, Seven Gibson, who professes a Melungeon lineage from both maternal and paternal sides of his family, told of his theory of Portuguese ancestry. "In Portugal the people lived in the highlands and when they came into the county, they just moved to the highlands. And sometimes I have a tendency to agree because I'm at home when I'm sittin' on top of a hill."[20]

Before the American Civil War, some Melungeons were classified as "free persons of color" and had the right to vote. However, in the Tennessee Constitution of 1834, free Negroes and non-citizen male inhabitants were deprived of the right to vote.[21] Writing for the *Nashville Banner*, Aswell expounded upon the legal ramifications of putting this group into a second-class social status:

> This law [stated] that in the new State of Tennessee no free persons of color—meaning Melungeon[22]—could vote or hold public office. Furthermore, no free person of color could bear witness in court against a white man. In a word, the Melungeons were made legally helpless in any legal dispute involving a white man. If a white man claimed a Melungeon's property, the victim had no recourse. He must either vacate or be forcibly ejected by officers of the law.[23]

---

[20] Seven Gibson, interview with author, audio recording, 26 June 1999, in possession of author.

[21] Robert Shannon, ed., *Annotated Constitution of Tennessee* (Nashville: State of Tennessee, 1915) 374–75.

[22] Although the terms "free persons of color," "Mulattoes," and "Mustees" are found in the journal of the proceedings from the revised Constitution of Tennessee; the word "Melungeon" is not.

[23] James Aswell, "Lost Tribes of Tennessee's Mountains," *Nashville Banner*, 22 August 1937, 2.

The so-called "one-drop rule" specified that anyone born with a single drop of "Negro" blood would be considered a person of color.[24] As Azoulay put it, "It is not really the color of one's skin that matters, but the 'race' of one's kin."[25] Hollinger addresses this rule as depriving those with even a hint of black skin a choice in their ethno-racial affiliation, thereby making race unavoidably controlled by genealogy and not by culture. He argues that "defenders of cultural diversity need to take a step beyond multiculturalism, toward a perspective [he calls] 'postethnic'.... [This] postethnic perspective favors voluntary over involuntary affiliations."[26]

According to participants, the one-drop rule was quite convenient for the early Scotch-Irish settlers who were moving into the region expecting free expanses of rich bottomland to farm. Madonna Cook offers an explanation that is widely shared within the Melungeon community:

> When the first European settlers came, the Melungeon families had all the good river bottomland and were farming it, had been here for several generations. Then in the 1830s, the Tennessee legislature passed a law that said if you had 1/8 or 1/16 Negro blood, you could not own land, you could not vote, and you could not testify in court against a white man. And because the Melungeon people were of a darker complexion, they said, "Well, you must be of Negro heritage and therefore you can't own this land." And they took their land, put them off their land, and said, "You can't keep this," even though they were there when the original Europeans came. So what was left was to go up the ridges to the poor land, the rocky soil, where

---

[24] For further discussion on this topic, see Lawrence Wright, "One Drop of Blood," *New Yorker*, 25 July 1994, 47; James Davis, *Who is Black?: One Nation's Definition* (University Park: Pennsylvania State University Press, 1991).

[25] Katya Gibel Azoulay, *Black, Jewish, and Interracial: It's Not the Color of Your Skin, but the Race of your Kin, & Other Myths of Identity* (Durham: Duke University Press, 1997) 4.

[26] David Hollinger, *Postethnic America: Beyond Multiculturalism* (New York: BasicBooks, 1995) 2–3.

there was not good farming. But they went and they eked out an existence with whatever they could, whether it was digging ginseng or making, some of them made moonshine and sold it, whatever they had to do to make a living, they did. But they did have good land in the early 1800s and it was taken away from them.[27]

It stands to reason that if Melungeons were among the first settlers in the region, they would have claimed the prime bottomland rather than trying to eke out a living by farming mountaintop ridges. However, the Scotch-Irish migration into southwestern Virginia/northeastern Tennessee occurred nearly 100 years before the enactment of the Tennessee law referred to by the participant. Rehder claims that by 1735, Scotch-Irish settlers had moved into southwestern Virginia: "The majority of early settlement focused upon the favorable soils and slopes adjacent to the Great Valley.... Only later did settlement expand to areas of lesser soil quality, steeper slopes and greater isolation."[28] According to Everett, the first Melungeons entered and settled the area at the Virginia/Tennessee border along Newman's Ridge between 1802 and 1804.[29] Nonetheless, although they may not have been forced out by the "one-drop" rule, it seems probable that these Melungeons faced discrimination because of their mixed ancestry and, as a result, settled in isolated communities or migrated to regions where their heritage was not suspect.[30] Speaking of her husband's great-grandfather, Madonna stated that "he had his land taken away in the 1830s and the next generation or two, the family just... they went from being landowners and substantial citizens to very, very poor."[31]

[27] Madonna Cook, interview with author, audio recording, 28 June, 1999, in possession of author.

[28] John. B. Rehder, "The Scotch-Irish and English in Appalachia," in *To Build in a New Land: Ethnic Landscapes in North America*, ed. Allen Noble (Baltimore: The Johns Hopkins University Press, 1992) 100.

[29] Everett, "Melungeon History and Myth," 372–73.

[30] See Edward Price, "The Melungeons: A Mixed-Blood Strain of the Southern Appalachians," *The Geographical Review* 41/2 (April 1951): 256–71.

[31] Cook, interview with author.

The competing versions of history and identity help demonstrate the significance of imagined history and its historical importance within the Melungeon community. Berger and Luckmann say identity is formed by social process, that it is "a phenomenon that emerges from the dialectic between individual and society."[32] To a certain extent, the Melungeons have been both culturally constructed and self-defined. "By defining itself, ethnically or otherwise," explains Fitzgerald, "a group escapes classification by others."[33] Perhaps this is the objective of self-definition and the direction in which the Melungeon community is headed. By becoming the authors of their own Internet Web sites and listservs, Melungeons have begun to actively embrace Hollinger's postethnic ideal of "voluntary over involuntary affiliations."

Red, White, and Black

In my initial interviews, it immediately became apparent that many of the participants gladly embraced their Native American genealogy while avoiding any mention of African heritage. Not surprisingly, the number of Americans who identify with American Indians on US census forms has risen 259 percent from 1960 to 1990.[34] Promises of entitlement from the federal government and America's move toward a more positive attitude concerning minorities are likely reasons for this increase.

Barbara Langdon spoke of her great-grandfather being a Native American Cherokee and how her mother and sisters always spoke about it.[35] Nancy Sparks Morrison also spoke of having Native American ancestry: "I had a grandmother, a great-grandmother who I knew. She said that she was quarter strain Indian, I think she said Cherokee."[36] As Seven Gibson drove me around Newman's Ridge (outside of Sneedville,

---

[32] Peter Berger and Thomas Luckmann, *The Social Construction of Reality: A Treatise in the Sociology of Knowledge* (New York: Doubleday, 1966) 160.

[33] Thomas Fitzgerald, "Media and Changing Metaphors of Ethnicity and Identity," *Media, Culture & Society* 13/4 (1991): 202.

[34] Wright, "One drop of blood," 47.

[35] Barbara Langdon, interview with author, audio recording, 26 June 1999, in possession of author.

[36] Nancy Sparks Morrison, interview with author, audio recording, 18 June 2004, in possession of author.

Tennessee) pointing out legendary landmarks on the Melungeon heritage trail, I casually questioned him on Melungeon ethnicity. He explained that there was some misunderstanding on the issue of race. He felt that the "black" component stemmed from the Black Hawk War or some other Native American connection.[37] In fact, the word "black" was often used euphemistically when participants spoke of their ancestry. Barbara Langdon explains: "They would say they were Black Dutch or Black Irish, or French, or Native American. They'd say they were anything but Melungeon because anything else would be better...because to be Melungeon was to be discriminated against."[38] Seldom would a participant even recall hearing the word Melungeon in connection with their family heritage. As Judy Bill remembered, "We thought we were Black Dutch. We were told we were. My great grandfather said he was Black Dutch and he said his father was Black Dutch." When I asked Judy what that meant, she replied, "Nobody ever knew, nobody knows today. There's no such thing as Black Dutch I've learned, you know, so if I'm not Black Dutch, what in the world was I and it turned out I've got Melungeon connections. But, no, there's no such thing as Black Dutch."[39] Cleland Thorpe identified the "black" element in another way: "My own theories, you know, there is all sorts of theories about this so, I had some people from the Black Forest of Germany, yeah, sure enough."[40]

There were other names associated with the Melungeons, many of which could be construed as negative, although Mattie Ruth Johnson was careful to distinguish between Melungeons and African-Americans: "There were some around that obviously was darker skinned and I know one or two that was very dark. They did not have any Negro features whatsoever, but a lot of them were dark-skinned. They looked more

[37] Gibson, interview.

[38] Langdon, interview with author.

[39] Judy Bill, interview with author, video recording, 30 June 1999, in possession of author.

[40] Cleland Thorpe, interview with author, audio recording, 26 June 1999, in possession of author.

Indian maybe or could be more Portuguese as we're finding out now."[41]
This last statement begs the question, what does a Portuguese look like?
It appears that some Melungeons could not identify themselves as being
part African, but still found it necessary to associate their identify with
some outsider group. It even became necessary to invent a group such as
the "Black Dutch" rather than identify with the unequivocal "other"
within American society. As Barker informs us, "Identities are wholly
social constructions and cannot 'exist' outside of cultural
representations…identity is not an already existent 'fixed thing,' a
possession of the self; rather, identity is a constitutive description of the
self in language."[42]

Claude Collins recalls the use of the word Melungeon specifically as
a derogatory term: "It was just a bad word. Parents would tell children
that the Melungeons were going to get you and carry you away."[43] There
were also some self-identified Melungeons who used the name in a less
than positive manner. Mattie, who grew up on Newman's Ridge[44]
(where she believes the Melungeons first colonized), spoke of how "we
had a habit of calling each other an old Melungeon and other names.
People on the mountain did that."[45]

When Mattie spoke of going into town as a child, she recalled being
referred to as one of "those little ridgemanauts." Still others would refer
to them as "Ramps."[46] A ramp is a plant that grows wild in the southern
Appalachian Mountains. It has a garlicky-onion flavor and a very
pungent odor. It was sometimes said that Melungeons harvested and ate
the plant and the overpowering odor caused them to smell of ramps. Alta
Porter, who grew up near Stone Mountain (outside Wise, Virginia),
remembered calling the people who lived on the ridges "Ramps." She

---

[41] Mattie Ruth Johnson, interview with author, audio recording, 18 June 2004, in
possession of author.

[42] Chris Barker, *Television, Globalization and Cultural Identities* (Philadelphia:
Open University Press, 1999) 31.

[43] Claude Collins, interview with author, audio recording, 18 June 2004, in
possession of author.

[44] Newman's Ridge is just outside of Sneedville, Tennessee.

[45] Johnson, interview with author.

[46] See Berry, *Almost White*, 34.

and her husband Lloyd Porter spoke of how the Melungeon community was viewed:

> Alta: Well, a lot of the people live here back in Stone Mountain, we call it, but they didn't call them Melungeons, they called them Stone Mountain Ramps. Anyway, and they were really looked down on but I wasn't aware of why.
>
> Lloyd: They was a little bit dark-skinned.
>
> Alta: Yeah, very much.
>
> Lloyd: And people didn't associate with them very much, did they?
>
> Alta: No. They were shunned.
>
> Lloyd: But I never heard anything bad about those people, we just called them Stone Mountain Ramps, we didn't mean anything by that, you know, back then.
>
> Alta: Well, it wasn't a nice thing to be called.
>
> Lloyd: No it wasn't, but when we were doing that, I didn't think anything bad about it.[47]

The external derogatory constructions of Melungeon identity were paralleled in some participants' words by evidence of internalized marginality. Campbell says that today we live in a demythologized world, and as a result, we make up myths ourselves.[48] Given the discrimination experienced by some Melungeons, specifically as "people of color," it is not surprising that a socially constructed mythology was established. As laws were enacted to displace, oppress, and marginalize the group, some participants appeared to internalize their marginalization. This is evident when Cleland speaks of his father: "I never saw my dad any time in my life that I can remember outside working or anything else but what he did not have a long-sleeved shirt on."[49] As a reaction to being discriminated against because of his darker

---

[47] Alta and Lloyd Porter, interview with author, audio recording, 1 July 1999, in possession of author.

[48] Joseph Campbell, *The Power of Myth* (New York: Doubleday, 1988).

[49] Thorpe, interview with author.

skin, Cleland's father would avoid exposure to the sun in hopes of controlling how he was viewed. In *Hunger of Memory*, Rodriguez addressed complexion and how his skin would not redden in sunlight, but became progressively dark. As a boy, his mother would warn him about being in the sun too long: "'You look like a *negrito*,' she'd say, angry, sorry to be angry, frustrated almost to laughing, scorn. 'You know how important looks are in this country.... You won't be satisfied till you end up looking like *los pobres* [the poor] who work in the fields, *los braceros*' [men who work with their arms]."[50] However, Rodriguez speaks of his dark complexion as assuming its significance from the context of his life. When he checks into hotels in Europe during winter months, the clerk might wonder if he has just been to the Caribbean: "My complexion becomes a mark of leisure."[51] Had he entered through the service entrance, his complexion might have labeled him as "disadvantaged." Rodriguez saw himself as being different from "los braceros" because of what he called "an attitude of mind, my imagination of myself."[52] However, as with the previous example of Cleland Thorpe's father, other Melungeons appeared to have negatively internalized their marginalization. For instance, Eliza Collins described her children's complexion: "I've got one kid that's the darkest child I had. We told him the sun tans him. Anyone that's dark-skinned, they're easy tanned in the sun. We would say that he took back after Papaw, that's all we'd say. But, we never quarreled or did nothin' about that. It's somethin' you never discussed."[53]

Rodriguez recalls how joyous his aunts were when speaking of having light-skinned children. His aunts regularly applied potions of lemon juice and egg whites to dark-faced cousins or would risk miscarriage by taking large doses of castor oil before giving birth. The

---

[50] Richard Rodriguez, *Hunger of Memory: The Education of Richard Rodriguez: An Autobiography* (Boston: D. R. Godine, 1982) 113.

[51] *Ibid.*, 137.

[52] *Ibid.*, 138.

[53] Eliza Collins, interview with author, audio recording, 19 June 1999, in possession of author.

results, they hoped, would be fair-skinned children.[54] Although Rodriguez speaks of hearing racial slurs in public (an uncle was once told to go back to Africa), nothing heard outside his house regarding skin color, he recalls, impressed him as much as hearing his aunts discuss his dark-skinned cousins.

In attempting to identify with "los gringos," Rodriguez remembers one of his mother's friends "who regarded it as a special blessing that she had a measure of English blood [and] spoke despairingly of her husband, a construction worker, for being so dark."[55] In searching for her roots as a child, Barbara Langdon told a similar story:

> I remember asking her [my grandmother] one time, kids at school were talking about nationalities, you know, what nationality are you? And I came home and I was asking what nationality we were and we were supposed, I think we probably were supposed to talk to our grandparents or something, so I asked my grandmother what nationality we were and she said, this is horrible what she said, but anyway, what she said was, well you know your grandfather [her husband], was Irish and she says, you know that good strong Irish blood eats up any of the bad stuff, so don't you worry about it, you're Irish and, yeah, and so I kind of grew up with this Irish sense, that that was my culture, and then when I went to do the research I discovered that I have Melungeon, but the grandfather that she claimed was, you know, purifying our blood, was really only half Irish and that was it. That was all the Irish there is in the family.[56]

As with many groups who have been discriminated against, some Melungeons left their homes for other regions of the country. Some moved to escape persecution, others simply left in search of better economic opportunities. However, issues of marginalization, both internal and external, followed them.

---

[54] Rodriquez, *Hunger of Memory*, 113.

[55] *Ibid.*, 116.

[56] Langdon, interview with author.

At the Unions, some Melungeons turned their internalized marginalization into a positive ethnic group identification that welcomed others, including myself. For example, because of my olive-colored skin, I was often assumed to be someone tracing his Melungeon heritage whenever I attended a Union. On more than one occasion, attendees would approach me and ask my last name in hopes of finding a link that would take them to a Melungeon surname missing in their family tree. When Darlene Wilson invited me to stay with her at her home, she would often introduce me as a "pseudo-Melungeon." In my copy of Brent Kennedy's book, *The Melungeons*, the author inscribed the message "To my dear friend who without a doubt is an *original* Melungeon!" When attending my second and third Unions, participants I had interviewed during the previous years' conferences would often run up to me with open arms as if greeting a long lost family member. Even the use of the term "union" in describing these gatherings conjured up images of a family reunion, as there was certainly a familiar feeling at each of these gatherings. In addition, I felt a palpable longing in the participants for connecting to one another, which brought to light the tie between the words common, community, and communication, as discussed by Dewey.[57]

In *Almost White*, Berry writes, "No one admits to being a Melungeon.... If you move among them, and win their confidence, an informant may tell you with a malicious glint in his eye that his next-door neighbor belongs to that worthless caste.... It is not a group one chooses to join, nor to which one takes pride in belonging. It is a caste, into which one is born and from which one escapes only surreptitiously."[58] It has been over forty years since these words were written. Certainly at the yearly Melungeon Unions, most attendees I interviewed relished their new-found ethnicity. Hollinger says, "A postethnic perspective challenges the right of one's grandfather or grandmother to determine primary identity. Individuals should be allowed to affiliate or disaffiliate with their own communities of descent

---

[57] John Dewey, *Democracy and Education: An Introduction to the Philosophy of Education* (New York: The Macmillan Company, 1916).

[58] Berry, *Almost White*, 39–40.

to an extent that they choose, while affiliating with whatever nondescent communities are available and appealing to them."[59] As previously noted, there were some participants who relished the idea of belonging to a somewhat exotic group. There were others within the Melungeon community, however, who did not welcome the attention. Given the group's history of being marginalized, this fact is easily understood.

Mining Oral Histories

In my interviews with Melungeons, individual stories of discrimination were told by numerous participants, many of which are impossible to verify. However, a number of them told versions of a single story that also appear in the published work of Will Allen Dromgoole, whose stories of her encounters with Melungeons are still identified as examples of racial prejudice. However, the story may have its roots in Melungeon memory and myth. According to Dromgoole's story:

> Somewhere in the eighteenth century, before the year 1797, there appeared in the eastern portion of Tennessee, at that time the territory of North Carolina, two strange-looking men calling themselves "Collins" and "Gibson." They spoke in broken English, a dialect distinct from anything ever heard in that section of the country. They claimed to have come from Virginia and many years after emigrating, themselves told the story of their past.
>
> These two, Vardy Collins and Buck Gibson, were the head and source of the Malungeons in Tennessee. With the cunning of their Cherokee ancestors, they planned and executed a scheme by which they were enabled to "set up for themselves" in the almost unbroken territory of North Carolina.
>
> Old Buck, as he was called, was disguised by a wash of some dark description, and taken to Virginia by Vardy where he was sold as a slave. He was a magnificent specimen of physical strength, and brought a fine price, a wagon and mules, a lot of

---

[59] Hollinger, *Postethnic America*, 116.

goods, and three hundred dollars in money being paid to old Vardy for his "likely nigger." Once out of Richmond, Vardy turned his mules' shoes and struck out for the Wilderness of North Carolina, as previously planned. Buck lost little time ridding himself of his Negro disguise, swore he was not the man bought of Collins, and followed in the wake of his fellow thief to the Territory. The proceeds of the sale were divided and each chose his habitation; old Vardy choosing Newman's Ridge, where he was joined by others of his race, and so the Malungeons became a part of the inhabitants of Tennessee.

This story I know to be true. There are reliable parties still living who received it from old Vardy himself, who came here as a young man and lived, as the Malungeons generally live, to a ripe old age.

The names "Collins" and "Gibson" were also stolen from the white settlers in Virginia where the men had lived previous to emigrating to North Carolina.[60]

This story of Melungeons passing as black was told to me on numerous occasions both by participants claiming Melungeon heritage and by those who had no Melungeon ancestry but grew up in either Sneedville, Tennessee, or Wise, Virginia. Johnnie Rhea, a seventy-five-year-old participant I first met at the Melungeon Heritage Association's genealogical workshop and considered by some to be a matriarchal figure within the organization, claims both characters in the story to be her grandparents. She elaborates on the information that to pass as African American, her ancestors stained their skin:

> One of my grandfathers sold the other 'un for a slave. My Grandpa Collins sold my Grandpa Gibson for a slave. He got a

---

[60] Will Allen Dromgoole, "The Malungeon Tree and Its Four Branches," *The Arena* 3 (June 1891): 472-473, quoted in Kennedy, *The Melungeons*, 93–94. Although admitting that some of the story may be true, Kennedy finds most of Dromgoole's conclusions "shortsighted, naïve, and certainly racist in nature," 94. A similar story is found in Ball, *The Melungeon*, 83–84.

team of horses, $200 in money, some goods, a wagon…must have brought in pretty good. They painted him with pokeberries, painted his face and hands with pokeberries and walnut stain…mixed it together and made 'em a paint and painted him. And so, they made up where they'd meet back. They painted Shepherd Gibson, put that paint on him and they sold him and they made a place where they'd meet back after they sold him. So they said they'd give him so long to get away from there. Well, he did. He eased out and washed it off and he said, "I ain't no colored person. I'm a white person." And they couldn't hold him. He was a white person—they couldn't hold him. So, he left out for home and went back to Newman's Ridge, that's where they went to. We got a history, son, here. I don't know it all and I been there all my life. It's somethin' else.[61]

This story may be viewed as a collective strategy for accommodating and incorporating the racialization of Melungeon identity through the creation or internalization of collective memory and community myth-making.

On my second day in Sneedville, a man walked up to me and shook my hand. He told me that he remembered me from church services the previous night and volunteered to drive me around. After I explained to him that I was more interested in speaking to some of the local residents than sightseeing, he took me to the town barbershop. As I entered the smoke-filled barbershop, I was first introduced to the barber, who had previously been the county judge until a law was passed requiring all justices to be lawyers. The current county judge was also there playing the guitar. It was in the backroom of the barbershop where I interviewed Sam Hopkins.

Sam, a resident of Sneedville, but not a Melungeon, volunteered his version of Vardy Collins and Buck Gibson's story, although his

---

[61] Johnnie Rhea, interview with author, audio recording, 19 June 1998, in possession of author.

perspective appeared to center on what fine traders the Melungeons were:

> Now them Melungeons, they were good traders, the original ones was, you know. And I know there was a Gibson and a Collins and the Gibson was pretty black. Most of them had black hair, blue eyes, and so forth, you know, and so this Collins and this other one, they'd boil bark and then rub it all over that one, you know, and turned him; he had the complexion of a colored man and everything. And they had a slave trade up at Jonesville, Virginia and he'd take him up there to that, you know, and sell him. They say he got a team of mules and a wagon, one time and he'd get money, you know, and then at night, he'd go and wash all that off of him and come on home. I don't know how long they done that but I heard 'em.
>
> Question: They did this more than once?
>
> Oh yeah, they made money.[62]

Although not a Melungeon, Sam must have heard this story many times having lived his entire life in Sneedville. He appeared to have internalized it, adding his own comment on the Melungeon as a good trader. With his statement, "Oh yeah, they made money," I could not help but think of some anti-Semitic "double-dealing" sentiments. This seemed especially poignant since many Melungeon families living on Newman's Ridge prided themselves on living off the land and would go into town only to trade animal hides or ginseng for staples they could not produce themselves. To add credence to his story, the participant added a specific geographical location for the slave trade.

There is no way of documenting the validity of the Vardy Collins and Buck Gibson story. The story, however, reveals other, more important things about modern Melungeon identity. As Portelli says, "Oral sources...are not always fully reliable in point of fact. Rather than being a weakness, this is however, their strength: errors, inventions, and

---

[62] Sam Hopkins, interview with author, audio recording, 28 June 1999, in possession of author.

myths lead us through and beyond facts to their meanings."[63] Although Kennedy found Dromgoole's conclusions racist in nature, the adoption of the story by a participant claiming to be a direct descendent of the characters speaks to the acceptance of the story within the Melungeon community and hints not only at the discrimination felt by the group, but also at the identification with an "other" oppressed group.

When approaching oral history, it is often memory that is the rub. Lowenthal tells us how historians rely on historical records to be stable, whereas we expect "memory" to mislead us.[64] Yet to an oral historian, falsehoods can say as much as truths. A false statement can still be viewed as psychologically true and may be viewed as more important to the community than the truthful version of events (see Portelli below). When a myth is repeatedly told within a society, it often ends up being accepted by the society. Oral histories can tell us not only about the events that occurred but also of the psychological costs to the people involved. This is something the written document cannot necessarily supply.

Thompson calls certain historians prejudiced when they call the written source superior to oral material simply because a piece of paper constitutes a kind of primary evidence that some view as being in an unbiased, pure form.[65] When Portelli examined the newspaper reports of the death of steelworker Luigi Trastulli in the Milan *Corriere della Sera*, "Italy's then most important paper," the written report had Trastulli's name wrong (Alvaro instead of Luigi). As Portelli puts it, "Apparently, written sources are not always automatically reliable."[66]

Calvin Coolidge once observed that people from his hometown "remember some of the most interesting things that never happened."[67] Ritchie tells of how everyone relives the glory days by retelling stories of

---

[63] Alessandro Portelli, *The Death of Luigi Trastulli, and Other Stories: Form and Meaning in Oral History* (Albany: State University of New York Press, 1991) 2.

[64] David Lowenthal, *The Past Is a Foreign Country* (Cambridge: Oxford Press, 1985).

[65] Thompson, *The Voice of the Past*, 117.

[66] Portelli, *The Death of Luigi Trastulli*, 3.

[67] William Allen White, *A Puritan in Babylon, the Story of Calvin Coolidge* (New York: The Macmillan Company, 1938) vii.

the past. However, each telling of the story moves it further from reality. In addition to individual life stories, the oral historian must also be aware of the collective memory of a community.[68] Portelli's piece, *The Death of Luigi Trastulli*, demonstrates how people actually invent history. Through interviews with older steelworkers, the author points out that the shooting death of Luigi Trastulli, in 1949 Italy, would not likely have been of historical significance if it were remembered "right." The collective memory or myth moves the killing of the worker from a small anti-NATO rally to a major protest march against labor conditions at the steel mill. Portelli says that "oral sources are credible but with a different credibility. The importance of oral testimony may lie not in its adherence to fact, but rather in its departure from it, as imagination, symbolism, and desire emerge. Therefore, there are no 'false' oral sources."[69] As Thompson put it, memory is part of an active social process.[70]

The Vardy Collins and Buck Gibson "sold into slavery" story could be viewed as a metaphor for addressing the murkiness of Melungeon racial identity. The stories differentiate between Melungeons and African Americans, allowing Melungeons to shed the blackness attributed to them by non-Melungeons, while at the same time setting themselves apart from the whiteness of slave owners by tricking the white-defined slave system. The story explains and makes positive their racially ambivalent and ambiguous social position and identity while at the same time there appears a slightly socially dangerous and suspicious aspect to the stories which could be identified with "border-crossers." Darnton, for instance, addresses "things that slip in between categories, that straddle boundaries, or spill beyond borders [to] threaten our basic sense of order."[71] It could be argued that Melungeons were often seen by

---

[68] Donald A. Ritchie, foreword to *Memory and History: Essays on Recalling and Interpreting Experience*, ed. Jaclyn Jeffrey and Glenace Edwall (New York: University Press of America, 1994) v–xi.

[69] Portelli, *The Death of Luigi Trastulli*, 51.

[70] Thompson, *The Voice of the Past*, 117.

[71] Robert Darnton, "The Symbolic Elements of History," *The Journal of Modern History* 58/1 (March 1986): 223. See also Mary Douglas, *Purity and Danger: An Analysis of the Concepts of Pollution and Taboo* (London: Routledge, 1966).

non-Melungeon Appalachians as crossing borders (racially and socially) and threatening the established order. In fact, the very racial implications of Sam Hopkins's non-Melungeon rendition of the story on how Melungeons made money parallel certain anti-Semitic stereotypes that fall into the more socially dangerous and suspicious aspects of how "border-crossers" are viewed.

Today, however, Melungeons are beginning to embrace their diversity. Through their involvement with the Internet, they are becoming the authors of Web sites that define their identity. These issues surrounding the construction of identity will be further examined in the following chapters on electronic media usage in rural Appalachia.

Chapter Five

Listening to Radio in Rural Appalachia[1]

Crystal Sets

When radios first came to Appalachia, they were not exactly a community building, nor an identity building, phenomenon. Most people were too poor to buy good radios or even any radio at all.

In 1936, the United States Department of Agriculture's Chief of Radio Service wrote: "During the early days of the development of radio, farm families were among the leading investors in receiving equipment."[2] This was not the case within the most distressed areas of Appalachia. "You know times was hard," commented Dulcie Reinhart. "Everybody worked hard at that time. I don't remember anybody back then who had a radio where we lived. I enjoyed it, yes I would have liked to have a radio, it's just we couldn't get it. Mom and Dad was lucky to have stuff on the table, there were nine children."[3]

---

[1] Material from this chapter has appeared previously in Jacob J. Podber, "Radio's Early Arrival in Appalachia: A Harbinger of the Global Society," in *Global Media Studies: Ethnographic Perspectives*, ed. Patrick D. Murphy and Marwan M. Kraidy (New York: Routledge Press, 2003) 184–212 and "Early Radio in Rural Appalachia: An Oral History," *Journal of Radio Studies* 8/2 (Winter 2001): 388–410.

[2] Morse Salisbury, "Radio and Country Life," *Rural America* 14/2 (February 1936): 17–18.

[3] Dulcie Reinhart, interview with author, video recording, 19 June 1998, in possession of author.

Still, participants, regardless of income, were resourcefully determined to join the radio revolution. Ida Mae Stoneburger recalled, "I remember when I was married in 1931. We was very poor and we traded five hens and roosters for a radio."[4] Buying a radio during this period was considered a major purchase. During the 1930s, the average yearly salary in the United States was $1,368.[5] However, in a region where most were farmers and miners, income levels were considerably lower than that. For example, a coal miner's yearly income for 1933 was $900.[6] Of course, the cost of living during the 1930s was considerably less than it is today. A new Ford automobile could be purchased in 1930 for $495 and a movie ticket was $0.35–$0.50.[7] But radios were not cheap. In 1930, the average radio cost $78. As set production increased to meet the demands of more radio owning households, the average cost of a receiver dropped to $55 in 1935.[8] Spending $55–$78 for a radio was a considerable amount for a nonessential commodity, and many within the region simply could not afford to purchase their own sets. Some, like Paul Weaver, made their own sets:

> The first one we owned was the one I made out of an oatmeal box and you'd wrap a wire around it so many times, and it was called a crystal set. I copied it out of the *Popular Mechanics* magazine. The reason that I didn't keep making radios, after the three tube come out with a speaker on it [is because] by that time I'd have had maybe $8 to $10 in it and I didn't have that. We never was without food nor clothing but we didn't have any money to jingle in our pockets either.[9]

---

[4] Ida Mae Stoneburger, interview with author, video recording, 17 June 1998, in possession of author.

[5] Lois Gordon and Alan Gordon, *American Chronicle: Seven Decades in American Life 1920–1989* (New York: Crown Publisher, 1990).

[6] Scott Derks, ed., *The Value of a Dollar: Prices and Incomes in the United States 1860–1989* (Detroit: Gale Research, 1994).

[7] Gordon and Gordon, *American Chronicle*, 89.

[8] Christopher Sterling and John Kittross, *Stay Tuned: A Concise History of American Broadcasting* (Belmont CA: Wadsworth Publishing Co, 1990).

[9] Paul Weaver, interview with author, video recording, 19 June 1998, in possession of author.

Crystal radios required no power source and were unable to amplify incoming signals, thereby requiring the use of headphones. What followed were tube radio sets that required a power source, usually a wet cell battery. Later models were powered by dry cell batteries and electricity.

Not all crystal sets were homemade. Some participants, like Frank Frazel, had pre-fabricated sets: "I had a manufactured crystal set that I got from my dad and it was the type that you would hook to the bed springs in the bed. By the time I got it, it was an antique. The springs worked as an aerial."[10] Besides needing a bedspring (or some other aerial), there were definite limitations to crystal sets. Edger Smith remembered the early crystal sets: "You had the earphones, the headphones on your ears. And I'd use them too, but there was ten of us kids, five girls and five boys and it was busy all the time. Someone was listening on it all the time. I wasn't very old, I was five or six years old at most although I really enjoyed listening to it."[11] Ida Mae recalled her brother getting a crystal set: "You had to put the earphones on to listen to it and we had to fight over the earphones to see who got to listen."[12] Clyde Pinney spoke of visiting his grandparents: "My grandfather, who was a Baptist minister, was also an avid fight fan. The first radio they had was a crystal set with earphones, and Grandpa and my dad would share the earphones and the rest of the people would talk while Grandpa and Dad listened to the prizefight on the radio."[13] Given the expense of tube or console radios, it was understandable that many within this poor region of the United States first listened to crystal radio sets even as late as the 1930s.

In 1933, at the age of sixteen, Henry Shaffer went to work in the coalmines for $13 a week: "Of course Dad dealt with the company store

---

[10] Frank Frazel, interview with author, video recording, 19 June 1998, in possession of author.

[11] Edger Smith, interview with author, video recording, 17 June 1998, in possession of author.

[12] Stoneburger, interview with author.

[13] Clyde Pinney, interview with author, audio recording, 25 June 1998, in possession of author.

so he never got no pay check. So in order to get any money, I started working at the mine. Then we'd use my money to go buy things that we wanted."[14] The establishment of the company store by coal mining corporations exacted powerful social controls over miners and led to economic exploitation. If miners wished to draw on their pay before their monthly or bi-monthly payday, scrip was issued. Printed by the coal mining company, scrip could only purchase goods from the company store. Given that the miner paid the company for his housing, mining explosives, and tools, there was often little left for purchasing anything other than bare essentials.[15] As Henry put it, "We had to buy our own powder, we had to buy the carbide lights, we had to buy the tools to work with. The company furnished the coal for us to dig out."[16] Only with Henry's second paycheck were the Shaffers able to be the first family in the "holler" to get a console radio.

Although Ong describes radio as an orally-based medium that "has brought us into an age of 'secondary orality' [with] its fostering of communal sense,"[17] it is interesting to note that he was presumably speaking of radio transmitted over a speaker that could be listened to by a group. Yet these early radio enthusiasts who listened to broadcasts on headphones were in fact isolated from those around them because of their immersion in their own auditory experience. In effect, these headphone-wearing listeners were as isolated and closed off as readers of printed text. Ong might have described them as members of "the individualized introversion of the age of writing."[18] Unlike the communal experience participants often cite in listening to radio, these early examples seem to be antithetical to communal listening.

---

[14] Shaffer, interview with author.

[15] Laurel Shackelford and Bill Weinberg, eds., *Our Appalachia* (New York: Hill and Wang, 1977).

[16] Shaffer, interview with author.

[17] Walter Ong, *Orality and Literacy: The Technologizing of the Word* (London: Metheun, 1982) 136.

[18] Walter Ong, *Rhetoric, Romance, and Technology: Studies in the Interaction of Expression and Culture* (Ithaca NY: Cornell University Press, 1971) 285.

Batteries Powered the Early Radio Sets

Another obstacle stood in the way of communal use when radio was first introduced. When people speak of listening to radio in Appalachia during this period, they are speaking of battery-powered radio because most rural household in the region had no electricity during the 1920s, 1930s, and 1940s. In the 1930s, the Rural Electrification Administration (REA) began bringing electricity to rural areas of the nation.[19] But for many people in rural Appalachia, electricity did not reach their homes until the 1950s or later. For instance, in looking at Appalachian counties in Ohio, according to the Ohio Rural Electric Cooperatives, "Ohio cities had enjoyed the benefits of electricity for several decades prior to 1935. But only two Ohio farms out of ten were electrified by 1935 and, for the most part, those were farms close to towns and existing power lines."[20] Although rural electric cooperatives started to appear in Ohio in 1935, much of the four most economically distressed counties within the Appalachian region of the state were not wired. For instance, only tiny northeastern and southwestern corners of Athens County were served by the Rural Electric Cooperative that provided electrical power to the area. Approximately 50 percent of Meigs and Morgan County were electrified.[21] Although Vinton County was included in its entirety within the Buckeye Rural Electric Cooperative Service Area, not all residents in the county had electric power in their homes.

Because most participants lived on farms, the "rural farm" category in each census was chosen for this comparison. Although some participants spoke of living in coal towns, those locations were often as isolated as rural farm districts.

In the 1940 census, only 26.7 percent of rural farm homes in Meigs County had "electric lighting." (One must assume from the "electric lighting" category that this meant electric service to the house rather

---

[19] Parker and Hudson, *Electronic Byways*, 127.

[20] Ohio Rural Electric Cooperatives, *The Light and the Power: Commemorating 50 Years of Electricity in Rural Ohio* (Columbus: Ohio Rural Electric Cooperatives, Inc, 1985) iii. Because rural Appalachian Ohio was where I began my first interviews, I use Ohio's rural electrification history as an example.

[21] *Ibid.*

than a gasoline powered generator or a battery-powered home plant. Censuses earlier than 1940 made no mention of this category). There were 39.2 percent of Athens County rural farm homes with electric lighting and just 12 percent in Morgan County. Interestingly, Vinton County, the only county included in its entirety within a rural electric cooperative service area, had only 17.1 percent of its rural farmhouses electrified in 1940.[22] This is in contrast to 36.6 percent of all Ohio farm dwellings that were electrified by June 1937 and 78.8 percent of all dwellings in the United States with electric service by 1940.[23] By 1950, these numbers had increased dramatically. Rural farm houses in Meigs County were 88.2 percent electrified, Athens County had 84 percent of its rural dwellings electrified, Morgan had 77.9 percent, and Vinton had risen to 78.8 percent.[24]

Reasons for not having electricity ranged from economic barriers to residents' concerns over electricity's safety. As Edna Norris recalled:

When electricity first came to our area, the people were told of all the dangers...that lightning could run in on it, and they told people they needed a lightning rod for their house. So, the neighbors had a meeting and they got together and discussed whether we should have electricity or not because it was so dangerous. They said if you're even putting a bulb in, you could get shocked. So, we were a little scared about it. So when we finally got electricity I remember my dad the first time he had to change a light bulb. All of us went into the kitchen; we had to get way back and here's about seven or eight of us with our heads stickin' around the door watching to see if dad got

---

[22] US Bureau of the Census, *Sixteenth Census of the United States* (Washington, DC: U.S. Government Printing Office, 1940).

[23] Ohio Rural Electric Cooperatives, *The Light and the Power*, 17.

[24] US Bureau of the Census, *Census of Housing: 1950* (Washington DC: U.S. Government Printing Office, 1953).

electrocuted whenever he changed the bulb. You know, it was a scary process. I never will forget that.[25]

Given these limitations, participants' first radios, regardless of when they got them, were most likely battery powered. However, as some in the region started to purchase or trade for radios, many could not afford the wet cell battery that was required to operate it and were forced to use the one from their automobile. Edna told of some of the difficulties in removing the car battery when they wanted to listen:

My dad bought a radio and he would take the battery out of the car to run it. When we used it on Saturday nights, my dad would park the car up on the hill so when he put the battery back in the car we could shove the car down the hill to get it to run and re-charge the battery. You had to be careful where you were or you couldn't get the car started after using the battery for the radio. If you couldn't push the car to get started with the dead battery, you would have to get the mule to pull you.[26]

People were quite ingenious in devising ways of listening to the radio. Before getting a radio at home, Edna recollected going to listen at a neighbor's house: "The first radio I can remember was at a good friend's house, which was powered by a windmill on top of their house, and that charged the battery and kept the radio going."[27] Others built homemade generators. John Williams "rigged up a battery charger with a washing machine gasoline engine and a Model-T Ford generator."[28] Because of economic reasons, people used the radio only sparingly. Golda Hart recalled, "Of course you couldn't hear it for everything.

---

[25] Edna Norris, interview with author, video recording, 11 May 1998, in possession of author.

[26] *Ibid.*

[27] *Ibid.*

[28] John Williams, interview with author, video recording, 25 June 1998, in possession of author.

You'd play it and then you shut it off to save your battery."[29] Clyde Pinney added, "If there was anything important coming along that we wanted to watch [sic], why the battery would be charged and we would keep it charged for that particular event. It wasn't just turn it on like we do today with our television and let it run all day. We took care of the amount of battery power that we had."[30]

When households were electrified, radio had become such an important part of people's lives that some had an electric set waiting. As Clyde recalled, "We bought an electric radio and had it setting on the shelf waiting for the electricity to be turned on. Whenever the electricity arrived, the radio was there waiting for it."[31]

Clear Channel Stations Bring the City to Rural America

Despite the obstacles, people's ingenuity and enthusiasm ensured a strong community reception for what the technology made available.

During radio's early years, the most powerful AM broadcasters were the clear channel stations that were authorized to broadcast at high power levels and granted exclusive use of their frequency at night. These stations enabled radio listeners to pick up programming from hundreds of miles away. This was especially important for people living in isolated, rural areas of the country.[32]

In 1962, *Broadcasting* magazine wrote:

> From 1930 to 1950—give or take a few years on either side—the clear channel stations reigned supreme. They were the big voices of the air.... Their programs and commercials rang loud and clear during the day, and rose to a roar at night.... It was these stations that carried the most popular programs, the national advertising—both network and national spot—that

---

[29] Golda Hart, interview with author, video recording, 2 June, 1998, in possession of author.

[30] Pinney, interview with author.

[31] *Ibid.*

[32] James Foust, "A History of the Clear Channel Broadcasting Service, 1934–1980" (Ph.D. diss., Ohio University, 1994).

brought to millions of listeners in rural America their only
nighttime service.[33]

Clear channel stations had frequency signal protection at night
from 700 to 750 miles and north central Appalachia's geographical
location placed it within the frequency protection zone of several clear
channel broadcasters. The introduction of the Federal Radio
Commission's 1928 frequency allocation plan was the first to allow a
handful of stations to broadcast on AM frequencies at the highest power
available: first 25,000 watts and later 50,000 watts. Other stations could
use these frequencies during the day but were forced off the air at night
to prevent interference with the clear channel stations. The purpose was
to provide service to ensure good reception for rural and remote radio
listeners. The Federal Radio Commission and later the Federal
Communications Commission agreed that this policy should be among
their most important concerns.[34]

Owners of clear channel stations formed the Clear Channel
Broadcasting Service (CCBS) to lobby for the protection of clear
channel policy. After the start of World War II, CCBS members wrote a
letter to President Roosevelt affirming the group's interest in keeping
rural and small town radio listeners informed: "As the nation's
independently owned clear channel stations, ours is a doubled
responsibility in radio during this crisis. Our audiences comprise not
only city listeners, but also the millions of Americans living on farms and
in small towns across the country. The principal radio voice reaching
some 50,000,000 rural and small town listeners must promote the
unified effort needed to win this crucial struggle."[35] Although there were
clearly economic motives behind this letter, one must also appreciate
how important it was to keep the entire nation informed during the war
years.

Because of their geographical isolation, rural communities may have
had the most to gain from these high-powered radio stations. Radio

---

[33] "Clear Tops for 20 Years," *Broadcasting*, 15 October 1962, 29.
[34] Foust, "A History, " 129.
[35] Quoted in *ibid.*, 129.

appeared to confirm Appalachia's connection to the rest of the nation and made them feel good about that connection. However, living in rural Appalachia did have its own quirks when it came to listening to the radio. Roy Cross remarked, "Down here you were so restricted, you couldn't get the Columbus [Ohio] station like BNS but you could get Atlanta [WSB], loud and clear."[36] Archie Greer also remembered listening to clear channel stations. "You didn't get a lot of radio back then in this area. You got WLW out of Cincinnati, that was a clear channel you could get on a good night. Also WJR out of Detroit. Of course, at night you could pick up a lot of stuff. You could pick up New York, Nashville, Boston, Atlanta."[37] Some spoke of the mountains as an aid to radio reception. As Cecil Webb recalled: "My daddy was interested in prizefights, but we couldn't pick up the station that broadcast those prizefights at home, so me and my dad would drive up to the top of the mountain and sit there in the car and listen to the fights."[38]

Sitting on the Floor Listening to The Opry, Prizefights, and The All-American-Boy

If there was one program that most participants mentioned listening to, it was the *Grand Ole Opry*. Before electricity came to the region, participants spoke of how they planned their radio usage to guarantee that the batteries would be charged on Saturday nights so they could listen to the *Grand Ole Opry*. As Irene Flowers recalls: "Saturday night was the only time we listened to radio. Daddy never went anywhere on Saturday. We only had a Model-A Ford and he would take the battery out on Saturday night and hook it up to the radio so he could hear the *Grand Ole Opry* and that was the only music we had, the only couple of three hours we could listen. We never did it no other night, just Saturday night."[39]

---

[36] Roy Cross, telephone interview with author, 24 February 1998.

[37] Archie Greer, telephone interview with author, 20 January 1998.

[38] Cecil Webb, interview with author, video recording, 11 May 1998, in possession of author.

[39] Irene Flowers, interview with author, audio recording, 13 May 1998, in possession of author.

The *Grand Ole Opry* went on the air in 1925, broadcast from Nashville's WSM radio station. Seventy-five years later, on 17 June 2000, the *Grand Ole Opry* went online, when the program was first Webcast on the Internet. Modeled after the *WLS National Barn Dance* from Chicago, the *Grand Ole Opry* was originally launched as the *WSM Barn Dance*. Radio stations across the South and Midwest had been broadcasting live country music since the early 1920s. Many attribute WSB in Atlanta with starting the trend and WBAP in Fort Worth, Texas, with originating the first radio barn dance. Before government regulations, WBAP's early barn dance programs out of Fort Worth were picked up as far west as Hawaii and as far south and east as Haiti.[40] The huge broadcast footprints of these clear channel stations allowed country music programming to gain popularity throughout most of the nation.

In 1927, the *WSM Barn Dance* followed NBC's *Musical Appreciation Hour*. When WSM's country music program went on the air, the announcer said, "For the past hour we have been listening to music taken largely from grand opera, but from now on we will present the *Grand Ole Opry*."[41] The name stuck and the *Grand Ole Opry* is now the world's longest running live radio program.

The *Grand Ole Opry's* predominance as the leading country music program was solidified in 1939 when NBC agreed to carry a thirty-minute segment each Saturday night on its national network. NBC affiliate stations across the country broadcast the show, thus allowing listeners outside of WSM's reception area to tune-in to the program. By being carried on a network, the show gained national status. However, the thirty-minute segment was only a portion of the four-and-a-half-hour program. True *Opry* fans, who were able to receive WSM, listened to the full program. Ivan Tribe recollected that "here in southeastern Ohio, just about everybody listened to WLW out of Cincinnati. At night, they did network shows. And we listened to WSM in Nashville a lot, and the *Grand Ole Opry*. People also listened to WLS in Chicago."[42]

---

[40] Bill Malone, *Country Music, U.S.A.* (Austin: University of Texas Press, 1985).

[41] George Hay, *Story of the Grand Ole Opry* (Nashville: Hay, 1953) 1.

[42] Ivan Tribe, telephone interview with author, 3 February 1998.

Variety shows featuring country music, sometimes referred to as "hillbilly music," were among the most popular regularly scheduled programs on early radio. However, when John Williams joined the Navy, he quickly found out that there were radio variety hours featuring something other than "country" music:

> When I went into the navy in 1943, about half of our group was from this part of Ohio, Kentucky, and Tennessee. The other half was from Chicago and Michigan and large cities. We had one radio in boot camp and *The Hit Parade* and the *Grand Ole Opry* were on at the same time and that caused a terrible fight because fifty percent wanted *The Hit Parade*, which played popular music and the other half wanted the *Grand Ole Opry*. I heard that someone purposefully damaged the radio so that it would put an end to the fighting.[43]

This ability to identify strongly with "country music" radio programming reflects on how Appalachians might have felt "included" with national shows like the *Grand Ole Opry*.[44] Many I spoke to also listened to the *WLS National Barn Dance* from Chicago, the *WLW Barn Dance* out of Cincinnati, WWVA's *Wheeling Jamboree* from West Virginia, and WNOX's *Midday Merry-Go-Round* from Knoxville. Given that most of these stations were clear channel stations, these programs could be heard over a large portion of the country. At night, for instance, the *Grand Ole Opry* could be heard all over the southeast and as far west as Texas. WWVA's *Wheeling Jamboree* blanketed the northeast as far as Canada, and *WLS's National Barn Dance* covered the Midwest.[45]

In addition to country music on the radio, many participants spoke of the importance of news programming. As with the *Grand Ole Opry*, Edger spoke of his father saving the radio battery to ensure being able to listen to informational programming: "My dad liked to listen to the weather report because he was a farmer. He wouldn't let anyone else

---

[43] Williams, interview with author.

[44] Malone, *Country Music*.

[45] *Ibid.*

take the radio. We kids couldn't listen to anything cause we had to save the battery for that report."[46]

Few mentioned President Roosevelt's fireside chats, except in passing, although listening to news reports of America's war efforts during World War II was a top priority. Rather than mentioning specific events, many participants spoke of the broadcasters who brought the news into their homes. Lowell Thomas, H. V. Kaltenborn, and Gabriel Heatter were often mentioned. Edger, however, spoke of how his mother became the newscaster in his family: "My mother always listened to the news, you know, and when my dad would come in he'd ask her if there was any news of the day and she could quote him everything just word for word what she'd heard on the radio, you know. What news was happening."[47]

Sporting events, especially the "big fight," seemed to be the perfect vehicle for early radio broadcasting. Legendary boxers such as Jack Dempsey and Gene Tunney came to fame just as radio began to make inroads into American homes. As special event radio broadcasts, championship prizefights were not to be missed. John and his uncle, however, were not so lucky:

> Boxing or prizefights was another big thing around Hope and Zaleski [Ohio]. I remember my uncle taking me, when we didn't have a battery, into Zaleski to hear some of the Joe Lewis fights. I remember Max Schmeling of Germany was a top fighter at that time. And there were quite a separate group that wanted Schmeling to win and others Joe Lewis. I know my uncle took me to a local store in Zaleski to listen to it but Lewis knocked Schmeling out before we got there.[48]

Baseball games were also mentioned as participants spoke of trying to pick up ball games, mainly from Cincinnati.

---

[46] Smith, interview with author.
[47] *Ibid.*
[48] Williams, interview with author.

Of course, early radio not only carried musical and sporting events, it captured the listeners' imagination with drama, soap operas, comedy, adventure, and religious programming. Seventy-year-old participants recalled their youth when they ran home from school to listen to soap operas such as *Stella Dallas*. Others, like Mary Rouch, spoke of "sitting on the floor with all the kids listening to *Amos 'n' Andy*, *The Lone Ranger*, *The Green Hornet*, and of course *Jack Armstrong*, you didn't miss *Jack Armstrong*, he was [giggle] the All-American-Boy!"[49]

Radio Created Important Social Gatherings

Many participants who didn't have radio at home spoke of going elsewhere to listen. Retired coal miner Henry Shaffer recalled: "The first memory I have is tuning in the Jack Dempsey fight. It was between 1925 and 1927.... There was a guy that had a radio, so I suppose there was forty or fifty people setting out in the yard, he had the radio on the porch."[50] Golda Hart recollected going to a neighbor's house:

> I remember back when we went to our neighbors; we wanted to hear what was going on in the world. That was back in the '30s, after I got married. I was just a farm girl you know. I married a farm boy, and we'd go to an older couple—they were such good friends of ours—and we'd listen to the *Grand Ole Opry* on Saturday night. And that was our Saturday night deal. She was a good pie maker and of course there would be snacks and pies. We didn't have a radio at home at that time.[51]

Getting together with neighbors and family to listen to the radio was an important social event and food—popcorn or pies—was often mentioned when recalling these get-togethers.

Many participants spoke of putting the radio on the porch to listen, although Bridget Marsh told of how her porch was not large enough to

---

[49] Mary Rouch, interview with author, video recording, 13 June 1998, in possession of author.

[50] Shaffer, interview with author.

[51] Hart, interview with author.

accommodate all her friends and relatives who wanted to listen to the first radio in the neighborhood:

> We had one of the first radios in our neighborhood, if you want to call it a neighborhood, because our nearest neighbor was like a half a mile out. But my dad cleared out the front yard and put the radio out and all the neighbors would come on Friday and Saturday evening to listen because we were the only ones that had a radio.... We had lots of relatives, probably sometimes twenty to thirty people would come. We didn't put it on the porch, no, we stayed outside under the trees. We wanted to be comfortable. It was like going to a drive-in almost, only under the trees.[52]

Like so many others, Bridget spoke of how family members had a specific job at these gatherings. Some would bring food and drink while the youngsters had a more onerous responsibility:

> Because we were related to everyone, of course, it was very friendly and lots of time my aunt would bring something, maybe a cake or something or a jug of tea or something.... We also had giant mosquitoes and stuff like that. We would always have to get the cow patty things to make a smoke for the night. That used to be my younger sister's duty. It's not offensive at all. My little sister would gather the thin dry ones, you know, we would light them and the smoke would keep the mosquitoes away. It always worked.[53]

During an era before air-conditioning, sitting outside under the trees or on the porch during the summertime was quite common. It not only kept one cool, it helped bring people together. As Bob Cole recalls:

---

[52] Bridget Marsh, interview with author, audio recording, 18 June 1998, in possession of author.
[53] Ibid.

I remember listening to radio, playing in the street and listening to news about the war. My parents, we didn't have air conditioning, so my parents would sit on the porch. The neighbors walked along the street and would stop and listen to the radio and then they'd discuss the news about the war or listen to the programs. The kids would play in the street while the adults sat on the porch, so there was a lot of interaction of people and everybody knew everything that was going on in the neighborhood.[54]

Certainly, people sat on their porches before radio. However, listening to the radio on the porch, especially during a national crisis such as World War II, seemingly brought people together, allowing them to voice their feelings and concerns about the war.

Just as most participants spoke of listening to the *Grand Ole Opry* every Saturday night, many spoke of listening to news broadcasts about the war each evening. Wanda Rose told of how it became a routine: "I remember back during World War II that at 9:00 at night we always listened to the news, you know, on the war, the war news. That was really important because there were so many people in service. We listened every night."[55]

By this time, radio had already begun to have a great impact on how people scheduled their time. In an area where outdoor activities were an integral part of social life, radio seemed to encroach upon that lifestyle. Lenora Pinney recalled how radio programming had an impact upon her father: "My dad was a foxhunter, he had a foxhound. And he and my brother would go fox hunting. At that time they used to call boxing, prizefights, so if there was gonna be a prizefight my dad would stay at

---

[54] Bob Cole, interview with author, audio recording, 26 June 1999, in possession of author.

[55] Wanda Rose, interview with author, audio recording, 22 June 1999, in possession of author.

home, he wouldn't go fox hunting, he would stay at home and listen to the fight."[56]

Listening to prizefights on the radio may have brought men indoors, but it still allowed for male bonding. Lloyd Porter recollected memories of his father and uncle:

> I don't know, it must have been about '30 or '32, something like that, I was about five years old or six, and a big fight was comin' on. I remember my uncle had a radio in the neighborhood. I don't know if anybody else had a radio or not. But my dad, and I guess maybe ten men in the neighborhood, was gathered around in this room around that radio and I went down to listen with them. Well, it was a show. I observed all of these old men, chewin' tobacco, sittin' around and spittin' and smokin' and it was a show when that fight came on. They were doin' this and that in their seats, you know, "ooh wowee," but the radio was fadin' in and fadin' out, you could hear something every now and then. And they were enjoying it. I didn't know what was goin' on, but I remember that stuck in my mind.[57]

Dancing to the radio was another cheap form of entertainment, even if it meant dancing in the streets. Henry tells of how "people went to the company store to listen to radio. The company store was open on Saturday night. People used to come down and they would try to dance in the road or do this or that, whatever they could do, 'cause on Saturday night there was no place to go anyhow."[58]

With "no place to go anyhow" and little cash, Saturday nights were usually spent listening to the radio. As Edna recalled, "You went to church on Sunday and prayer meeting on Wednesday night and that was

---

[56] Lenora Pinney, interview with author, audio recording, 25 June 1998, in possession of author.

[57] Lloyd Porter, interview with author.

[58] Shaffer, interview with author.

the only time you went out. So going to the neighbors on Saturday to listen to the radio was a big event."[59]

In an area in which geographical isolation fostered independence, strong family and community values were very important. Consequently, contrary to Riesman's "lonely crowd" theory, where electronic media was sometimes looked upon as an isolating force in society,[60] the arrival of radio in rural Appalachia appeared to enhance rather than disrupt family and community cohesion.

The Coming of Electric Power Dramatically Changed Listening Habits

The coming of electric power into the region dramatically changed the listening and, consequently, the social habits of rural Appalachians. With battery-powered radios, the entire family and visiting friends and neighbors would gather around the set to listen. As Lloyd recalled, "You couldn't listen to it, you couldn't turn the radio on unless everybody was there in the family."[61] The arrival of electricity into the region, however, allowed for a more casual interaction with the radio. Mendelsohn wrote that "generally speaking, radio functions as a diverting 'companion' and helps to fill voids that are created by routine and boring tasks."[62] Only with the arrival of electricity was the radio relegated to a secondary position. It no longer was the center of attention as listeners turned it on for music while dusting furniture or snapping beans for canning. Virginia Miller told how her uncle ran an electric wire down to his barn so he could "put on the radio while he was milking so there would be music for the cows, plus he could catch the news broadcast while he was milking. They said it would soothe the cows so they would give more

[59] Norris, interview with author.

[60] David Riesman, *The Lonely Crowd: A Study of the Changing American Character* (New Haven: Yale University Press, 1950).

[61] Lloyd Porter, interview with author.

[62] Harold Mendelsohn, "Listening to Radio," in *People, Society, and Mass Communications*, eds. Lewis Dexter and David White (New York: Free Press of Glencoe, 1964) 242.

milk and everything."[63] Electricity permitted the listener to turn on the radio whenever he or she wanted. There was no longer the need to save the battery for Saturday night and the *Grand Ole Opry*. As Lenora recollected:

> I remember when my brothers went to the service during World War II. My mom was always trying to get what was going on because she was concerned with their welfare. At that time we didn't turn it [the radio] on whenever we wanted to because, like I said, you had to save that battery. But now you just push a button and it comes on. So it's entirely different. I think you listen to it more now. Sometimes I'll just turn it on for the music while I do my work like dusting but not with the battery radio because you saved it for important things.
>
> Back then, after everything was done, you'd gather around the radio. It was real serious. You had to be quiet. My dad wouldn't let us laugh or giggle. It was serious business. They were really interested in what was going on.[64]

With the coming of electricity, female participants began to mention doing housework while the radio was on. When asked how electricity changed her life, Marian Dees compared her electric radio to the old crystal sets: "Sure it changed our habits 'cause it was there available all the time. It wasn't like that crystal set that somebody else had to handle. You could do it yourself, you could turn it on, it played a lot. My mother played it a lot. She would take her sewing basket and sew and we'd all gather around and listen to 'the stories.'"[65] The "stories," or soap operas, became an important diversion for many. Rhea Boring spoke of how they would "bring the green beans in, snap off those beans and get them ready for canning the next day while listening to 'the

---

[63] Virginia Miller, interview with author.

[64] Lenora Pinney, interview with author.

[65] Dees, interview with author.

stories' on the radio."[66] Although many participants spoke of doing work while the radio was on, some, like Pearl Borne, would give her full attention to her soap: "There was a soap at about two o'clock in the afternoon and I would quit work, whatever else I was doing, I'd quit everything to watch [sic] my soap."[67]

Others, like Bennie Lawson, didn't get electric power in their homes until the 1950s and used gasoline-powered generators to run the few electrical appliances they owned: "Our electric lights and iron was probably the only electric appliances we had because we didn't have electricity until I think about 1951 in the house I grew up in. We were real conservative about it. Mother had an electric iron so in order to listen to *Stella Dallas* there was no problem with me ironing in the afternoon so I could run the generator and listen to the radio.... I would iron so I could listen to the radio."[68] Although the radio was battery operated, both it and the generator were used sparingly because of economic concerns. Like many others without electricity, Bennie found ways to listen to her favorite programs.

Radio, arguably, was the first medium that connected rural Appalachia to the rest of the nation and to the world at large. In *The Radio Diary of Mary Dyck*, Pamela Riney-Kehrberg found that "radio connected rural people to the world beyond their farms in ways that no other medium of communication could."[69] Clyde agreed: "I would say radio broadened our horizons. You knew things that were happening all over the world rather than just in your immediate neighborhood. Even with the local newspaper, you're more or less limited to a small

---

[66] Rhea Boring, interview with author, video recording, 19 June 1998, in possession of author.

[67] Pearl Borne, interview with author, video recording, 2 June 1998, in possession of author.

[68] Bennie Lawson, interview with author, audio recording, 20 May 1998, in possession of author.

[69] Pamela Riney-Kehrberg, "The Radio Diary of Mary Dyck, 1936–1955: The Listening Habits of a Kansas Farm Woman," *Journal of Radio Studies* 5/2 (Summer 1998): 70.

geographical area. When radio came into being in this part of the country we could hear things from all over the world."[70]

Of course, motion pictures brought the world to residents of even the most rural communities. Because of their geographical isolation, however, getting to a town that could support a theatre was a big event. There were also concerns over cost, as taking a family to the movies was often prohibitively expensive for many within this region.

So, it was the radio that helped bring the world into the living rooms of rural Appalachia. As early as the 1920s, residents were able to identify with the regional country music programs broadcast on regional channels. In war time, clear channel broadcast stations were advocates of a national agenda that made sure residents of even the most isolated corner of the nation were electronically connected, thereby reinforcing ties to a national identity.

At the local level, Appalachia's regional "otherness"—its economic disadvantages and late electrification—affected the way radio was originally received in the region. When the region was electrified, being able to turn the radio on at any time changed the way participants interpreted, used, and interacted with the radio, thereby changing how this new medium affected their lives. In fact, it could be argued that the electrification of radio within rural Appalachia had as much of an impact on residents' lives as the arrival of the medium itself.

In addition, it appears that community cohesion, neighborhood social events, and individual ingenuity were among the main catalysts that helped Appalachians join the electronic media revolution that began with the advent of radio.

---

[70] Clyde Pinney, interview with author.

Chapter Six

Television in Rural Appalachia

The arrival of electric power in rural Appalachia had a dramatic impact upon the ways in which people experienced radio. No longer did residents have to ration battery power so that they could listen to a favorite program. Electricity assured that the radio could be turned on whenever the listener liked. But unlike early radios that were battery-powered (or, in the case of crystal sets, that required no auxiliary power), television had to wait for electricity. As Cleland Thorpe laughingly put it, "You can't watch television by candlelight. See, you got to get that electricity first."[1]

Although one participant, Margaret Sowers, spoke of first seeing television "in Macy's department store on a [high school] graduation trip to New York City in 1939,"[2] most interviewees had to wait until their houses were wired before seeing their first set. The first television sets went on public sale in the United States in 1938.[3] However, television goes back further than most people realize. In 1928, General Electric began semi-regular telecasts from its Schenectady, New York, labs, and NBC and CBS opened experimental TV stations in New York in 1930 and 1931, respectively. Of course, these telecasts were mostly for the benefit of a few engineers within the region who had receiving

---

[1] Thorpe, interview with author.

[2] Margaret Sowers, interview with author, video recording, 2 June 1998, in possession of author.

[3] Christopher Sterling and John Kittross, *Stay Tuned: A Concise History of American Broadcasting* (Belmont CA: Wadsworth Publishing Co., 1990).

equipment. NBC began transmitting more notable telecasts in 1938, including scenes from a Broadway play and the first live news report, a fire on Ward's Island (on New York's East River). It was at the 1939 New York World's Fair that NBC inaugurated its regular television service.[4]

Commercial TV began in 1941 when NBC and CBS were each granted a license by the Federal Communications Commission (FCC), although commercial television did not begin in earnest until 1948.[5] With America's entry into World War II, the FCC ordered a freeze (in early 1942) on new station construction to preserve electronic equipment for war needs. At the end of the Second World War, there were only six television stations on the air, each broadcasting just a few hours a day.[6] By the end of 1948, there were forty-eight. However, with the ever-increasing number of new license applications and only twelve VHF channels available to serve the entire United States, the FCC froze the processing of new television stations in September 1948. The freeze ended in April 1952 with the FCC's "Sixth Report and Order." In the report, the commission increased the number of available channels by adding seventy new UHF channels to the already existing twelve VHF channels. Over 2,000 allotments, with individual channels assigned to each of 1,291 communities, demonstrated a great increase over the prefreeze allotment of channels in only 345 cities. Two-thirds of the new allotments were UHF channels and approximately 10 percent of total channels were designated for noncommercial educational use, mostly in the UHF band.[7]

Nonetheless, UHF had a hard time competing with VHF throughout the 1950s. UHF transmitters cost more to install and

---

[4] Tim Brooks and Earle Marsh, *The Complete Directory to Prime Time Network TV Shows, 1946–Present* (New York: Ballantine Books, 1999).

[5] Michael Woal and Linda Woal, "Forgotten Pioneer: Philco's WPTZ, Philadelphia," in *Television in America: Local Station History from across the Nation*, ed. Michael Murray and Donald G. Godfrey (Ames: Iowa State University Press, 1996) 39–60.

[6] *Ibid.*

[7] Sydney Head, Christopher H. Sterling, and Lemuel B. Schofield, *Broadcasting in America: A Survey of Electronic Media* (Boston: Houghton Mifflin, 1994).

operate than VHF, and most television manufacturers continued to build primarily VHF-only receivers. Not until 1964 did Congress require manufacturers to equip all new television receivers with both VHF and UHF tuning. Today, there are more UHF stations than VHF stations in the United States, although VHF continues to enjoy a larger audience share. The tremendous growth of cable throughout the 1970s, 1980s, and 1990s had a great equalizing effect on UHF given that VHF and UHF signals are indistinguishable on cable.[8] The growth of DBS (direct broadcast satellite) has had a great impact on the variety of programming not to mention the quality of reception, especially in areas of the country where television broadcast quality may have been poor. This is immediately apparent by the numerous satellite dishes dotting the rural Appalachian landscape.

Television Comes to the Mountains

When Appalachians spoke to me of the anticipated arrival of television, they conveyed their great expectations at the time. Betty Dobbins remembered "reading in our *Weekly Reader*, when I was in first or second grade, about television and how wonderful we thought that was going to be, which it is."[9]

"It was 1951 when television came to the area,"[10] recalled Judy Bill:

> I was a little girl of eleven and my dad came home one day and he says, "Children, slick back your hair and wipe off your faces, I want to show you something." So, he piled my mother and him, my Aunt Pearl and six children in a Hudson and here we were all in the Hudson and he took us to a store where there was three televisions on display. First that he knew of because he kept abreast of anything new, you know, new innovations. We

---

[8] *Ibid*, 351-53.

[9] Betty Dobbins, interview with author, video recording, 2 June 1998, in possession of author.

[10] Participants I interviewed in the northeastern Tennessee/southwestern Virginia region spoke of picking up television signals from Bristol, Kingsport, and Johnson City, Tennessee.

parked the Hudson, the store was closed, but they left the TV sets going in these big glass windows and we thought it was fascinating. The kids sat on the hood to watch that television and some of us got outside and we just had a big ole time, you know, watching television for the first time. And a day or two later, my dad came home bringing a television because that was the thing to do.[11]

Perhaps more than any other event discussed, participants spoke of getting their first television set with remarkable detail. Virginia Miller remembers the day her family got theirs:

Oh, it was a big thing. My uncle had a television repair shop. We got this television [in 1954] and it had a weird-shaped screen on it and it stood about four feet tall and I was probably six or seven when we got the first television and I remember the day it came in, in this great big box and they brought it in. Uncle Paul brought it out in the back of his station wagon. And we were really amazed when it come on and we actually saw a picture on there.[12]

In the days before cable TV, poor reception was the rule rather than the exception in the "hollers." Participants seemed to spend as much time adjusting their aerials as watching programs. Madonna Cook recalled "real poor reception, couldn't see the images, but just to see anything, people just thought that was the greatest thing in the world. We were up there in the mountains and didn't get very good reception. And you get down behind that ridge and you lose everything. That's the way it's always been in these hills."[13] Lloyd Porter recalled his younger brother with what must have been the longest antenna cable in the world. "He was going all over the hillside trying to pick up a signal for that television, carrying it all over the mountain round. Once he got that

---

[11] Bill, interview with author.
[12] Miller, interview with author.
[13] Cook, interview with author.

signal, that was it, that was where you put the antenna."[14] Even when the antenna was in place, there were still adjustments to be made. "The first television in this community was at a neighbor's house," remembered Margaret Tabler. "Everyone would gather at their house to watch, but they had their antenna way up there on that hill, and the father would say, 'if you wanna watch it you gotta run up there on the hill to turn the antenna,' but we would get to watch the television."[15] Of course, being on top of a mountain ridge had its advantages. As Mattie Ruth Johnson recalled, "Being on the mountain, you could put up an antenna and pick up about five or six channels."[16]

The arrival of television in Appalachia also had many similarities with early radio's arrival. Many people were unable to afford the cost of a radio when they were first marketed; the same was true with television in the early 1950s. In mid-1948, the price of television receivers ranged from $375 for a five-inch screen to $500 for a seven-inch screen, which was several weeks' pay for the average worker. Just before WSB-TV took to the air in 1948, an Atlanta department store advertised a television receiver for $325, while "three cozy rooms" of furniture were advertised in the same paper for $295.[17] As with radio, while television set production increased, prices decreased. In the early 1950s, sets could be purchased for as low as $220, although depending on the size of the screen and other features, prices went as high as $800.[18] By 1954, a TV could be purchased for $140.[19]

"Just high dollar people had a radio," recalled Seven Gibson. "High dollar folk. That was another rare item, television was. Before we could get one, we walked to someone's house that had a TV and we'd watch

---

[14] Lloyd Porter, interview with author.

[15] Tabler, interview with author.

[16] Johnson, interview with author.

[17] Ginger Carter, "WSB-TV, Atlanta: The Eyes of the South," in *Television in America: Local Station History from across the Nation*, ed. Michael Murray and Donald G. Godfrey (Ames: Iowa State University Press, 1996) 79–105.

[18] Sterling and Kittross, *Stay Tuned*, 382-84.

[19] Scott Derks, ed., *The Value of a Dollar: Prices and Incomes in the United States 1860–1989* (Detroit: Gale Research, 1994).

Gunsmoke.... We'd walk up the road to a neighbor's house on Saturdays."[20]

Electricity and the Domestic Economy

Unlike the arrival of radio in a largely non-electrified rural Appalachia, the concurrent arrival of television and electricity in the region allowed for a more casual interaction with the TV. As Lull put it, "TV is a companion for accomplishing household chores and routines."[21] Edna Norris concurred: "Sometimes you would get yourself organized and sit down in the living room and peel potatoes or string the beans and get them ready for the next meal and watch television. You couldn't do the same with radio. It was electric that changed everything, since we had to use a battery for the radio, and it would always run down."[22]

Another important distinction between the arrival of radio and television can be demonstrated by looking at the domestic economy of television viewing in post World War II America. For example, Spigel examines the problems television posed for women's domestic chores. She writes, "The basic patterns of day-time television emerged as a distinct cultural form which entailed a particular set of female viewing practices."[23] To accommodate a medium that required more attention than radio, in 1952 the Western-Holly Company marketed the TV-stove, which allowed the "housewife" to watch her favorite program and her chicken roast simultaneously. Network executives, aware of how television could be incompatible with women's domestic labor, designed early soap operas with minimal action and visual interest, thereby allowing the housewife to listen to the program while performing housekeeping tasks in another room. Furthermore, the constant explanation of previous story lines in each episode allowed the

---

[20] Gibson, interview with author.

[21] James Lull, "The Social Uses of Television," *Human Communication Research* 6/3 (Spring 1980): 202.

[22] Norris, interview with author.

[23] Lynn Spigel, "The Domestic Economy of Television Viewing in Postwar America," *Critical Studies in Mass Communication* 6/4 (December 1989): 339.

homemaker to follow the plot and continue household work.[24] In an interview in 1951, ABC-TV vice-president Alexander Stronach said, "It's a good thing electric dishwashers and washing machines were invented. The housewives will need them."[25]

But even with electrification, some participants spoke of how the novelty of early television often resulted in viewing it with undivided attention. Bennie Lawson recalled getting her first television in 1956: "I remember watching *As the World Turns* in the afternoons. I didn't iron then, I just sat on the couch and enjoyed TV."[26] Madonna had similar memories of her mother watching soap operas:

> We had our first television in 1954, and *The Guiding Light* and *Search for Tomorrow*[27] would come on during the noon hour and they were fifteen minutes and they were live. My mother stopped everything in the house and went and watched those soap operas. You didn't talk, you couldn't get an answer out of her. She was just so, I think it was more television than it was the story, and she was watching it like you would a live play. You watch every moment, you don't want to miss something. It was just that it was a new thing and television was so new. So for fifteen minutes, well there was two right in a row, so there was thirty minutes that [she] did nothing but watch the live soap opera to see what was happening and who was doing what that day and it was just like it was people they knew. It was so serious.[28]

---

[24] *Ibid.*

[25] "All Day Long." *Newsweek*, 24 September 1951, 57. The concept of the postwar housewife needing labor saving appliances that create more leisure time, thereby allowing more time to be spent watching soap operas, appears to overlook one fact: buying into mass consumerism often requires a two income family, thereby eliminating the leisure time these appliances were presumably designed to produce.

[26] Lawson, interview with author.

[27] First telecast in 1951, *Search for Tomorrow* is considered the first soap to succeed on TV.

[28] Cook, interview with author.

Just as electrification eliminated the need to ration radio listening time, television's dependence on electricity quickly allowed the television set to become, after the initial novelty, a constant companion. Like many, Marian Dees had the television set on all day. She promptly began to use television as a companion and even as a babysitter when she left the set on in the living room for her kids while she cooked dinner in the kitchen: "I would watch anything. It went on when I got up in the morning, and it went off when me and the kids went to bed.... I never turned the television off, even when I went to the kitchen to cook. I would listen partly. But if I wasn't listening, the kids were while I was cooking."[29] When asked if radio changed her daily routine or habits, Francis Grim "didn't remember any habits changing, not until television came along. I remember our first television. I'd set in the front room with a dishpan of water to wash the dishes, and set there and watch television."[30]

The idea of taking a dishpan of water into the parlor to watch television might seem somewhat alien now. An avid viewer today would more likely purchase a set for the kitchen. Very few participants mentioned having more than one radio during the 1930s and 1940s. However, some participants spoke of having two TVs in the 1950s. In 1930, the average yearly salary in the United States was $1,368, and the average radio cost $78, which was 5.7 percent of a worker's annual salary. By 1954, the average annual salary had risen to $4,033, and a television set could be purchased for $140, or 3.4 percent of a yearly salary.[31] Although a large number of participants I interviewed were farmers and miners with incomes lower than the national average, purchasing power in the post-war era was certainly greater than during the Depression years of the 1930s.

Marian Dees spoke of her Quaker mother being so enthralled by television in the 1950s that her family purchased two sets:

---

[29] Dees, interview with author.

[30] Francis Grim, interview with author, video recording, 11 May 1998, in possession of author.

[31] Gordon and Gordon, *American Chronicle*, 27; Derks, *The Value of a Dollar*, 143.

Television must have changed my mother's life, too. I said she was a Quaker lady. She was very straight laced and in the beginning, television was a no-no, I mean it was something that wasn't allowed. But when she saw mine and saw there wasn't anything wrong with it, she got one. She watched it almost all the time but she and my father couldn't agree on what they wanted to watch so they got two of them. My father had one in the dining room to watch the ball games. Both my father and mother had their own television.[32]

Television and Religious Convictions

In a region where many residents have strong religious convictions, some participants addressed how content on television clashed with their faith. Nancy Jean Walker recalled going to her cousin's house:

In Appalachia, people were very religious and I remember if they [my cousin and her husband] were watching something on TV and a beer commercial come on, they would get up and turn the set off until that beer commercial went off because they didn't want that beer commercial influencing their family life or coming into their home. They might watch a ball game, but they would get up and turn the set off when the beer commercial came on.[33]

Tobacco was also against some participants' religious beliefs, but as a cash crop, many depended on it as a supplement to their income. Nancy Jean continues, "Um, I don't think there were any commercials besides beer that they found distasteful because most people grew tobacco and they didn't find the cigarette commercials, you know, distasteful so they wouldn't turn off the cigarette commercial."[34]

---

[32] Dees, interview with author.

[33] Nancy Jean Walker, interview with author, audio recording, 24 June 1999, in possession of author.

[34] *Ibid.*

Almost every Appalachian family I visited had some sort of garden. To a certain extent, the family garden was a cultural practice. For some, the garden was essential for providing a relatively varied menu. For others with more land to farm, cash crops such as tobacco provided additional income for the purchase of goods the family was unable to produce themselves.[35] Spending an afternoon with Seven Gibson illustrated how important cash crops were to many in the region. While in Sneedville, Tennessee, Seven invited me to ride with him as he did his daily errands. At his bank, Seven encountered a friend who asked for a cigarette. Seven indignantly told his friend that smoking was against his religion, to which his friend responded, "Well if it's against your religion, why do you grow tobacco?" "I've got to grow tobacco," Seven replied, "it's a cash crop!"[36]

Watching Early TV as a Community Activity

As with radio, early television seemed to bring people together. Just as some participants in Appalachia spoke of going to friends' and neighbors' houses to listen to prizefights on the radio, many also spoke of going to watch wrestling matches on TV at a neighbor's house. In his series of New York Times articles on television's impact on American society, Gould wrote, "The home has become a new center of interest for the most gregarious people on earth."[37]

Madonna Cook spoke of great gatherings to watch the first television in the community:

> I remember hearing about television. I didn't know what it was, but everybody was talking about it. I believe it was the principal of our school [who] got a television. And he was the

---

[35] In 2001, The New York Times called marijuana Appalachia's number one cash crop. See Francis X. Clines, "Fighting Appalachia's Top Cash Crop, Marijuana," New York Times, 28 February 2001, Kentucky edition, A10.

[36] Gibson, interview with author.

[37] Jack Gould, "TV Transforming U.S. Social Scene: Challenges Films," The New York Times, 24 June 1951, 1. Also, see subsequent articles in series dated 25, 26, and 27 June 1951.

first one in the community that had one that I can recall and he would have fifty people show up at his house to see TV. And I finally got to see television. It was a great social thing, a whole lot more than it is now, to gather together and watch a television program.[38]

In the 1950s, many television stations had limited broadcast hours. Some would not go on the air until the afternoon. Judy Bill remembered back to 1951 when her family was the first in the neighborhood to get a television:

> Some people hadn't even heard of it before. So they all gathered at our house, you know, and it didn't come on until four in the afternoon but they'd be there at three, you know, as soon as kids got in from school they'd change clothes and come on over to our house to watch TV. Back then, people visited each other, you know. We don't do that today. We get on the Internet to visit with each other, but back then it was okay if they came by and watched TV.[39]

As the first televisions arrived in the community, participants without TV spoke of paying long visits to households with sets. Lloyd Porter recalls his mother's concerned conversation with his father, Emmett Porter: "She said, 'Emmett, we gotta do somethin'. We gotta get a television because we're sittin' here by ourself. Our kids are all goin' somewhere else and watchin' television. We gotta get a television.'"[40] This strategy seemed to work. As Madonna remembered, "By the time we got a television a lot of people had it, but *Gunsmoke* was like ten Saturday nights. My brother would be back from a date on

---

[38] Cook, interview with author.
[39] Bill, interview with author.
[40] Lloyd Porter, interview with author.

Saturday night by ten so he could watch *Gunsmoke* with the family and pay full attention."[41]

As more and more residents spoke of getting a television set of their own, however, communal TV watching appeared to diminish. In fact, among some of the participants, there was a tendency toward over involvement on an individual level. For instance, wrestling captured the imagination of early television viewers, and some seemingly became overly absorbed in the new medium. Ruth McWhorton remembered watching with her brother and uncle: "My brother had a television and we'd watch wrestling. And I had an uncle and we'd have to hold him 'cause he'd get mad and try to go up and hit the television 'cause one of the wrestlers would do something bad and he'd try to hit the television. And we would have to hold him back from hitting the television."[42]

"Professional" wrestling programs became a regular form of entertainment on early live TV. As Erickson put it, "Because televised matches always managed to resolve themselves within the tight limits of '50s television, wrestling was the ideal 'sports event' of TV's first decade."[43] First telecast in the summer of 1948, NBC's *Wrestling from St. Nicholas Arena* was broadcast on Tuesday nights from 10 PM to 11 PM. During that same season, ABC telecast *Wrestling from Washington, DC* on Wednesday nights, and DuMont[44] telecast *Wrestling from Jamaica Arena* on Friday nights. DuMont's and ABC's wrestling programs were the two longest-running shows, staying on the air for nearly six years. In addition, there were syndicated wrestling shows such as *Wrestling from Hollywood*, which KTLA-Los Angeles began to distribute on film in

---

[41] Cook interview with author. In "The Social Uses of Television," Lull describes such an action as a relational/affiliation use of television, whereby television viewing is a convenient way of bringing families together.

[42] Ruth McWhorton, interview with author, video recording, 2 June 1998, in possession of author.

[43] Hal Erickson, *Syndicated Television: The First Forty Years, 1947–1987* (Jefferson NC: McFarland, 1989) 9.

[44] The fourth network, long before Fox, the DuMont Television Network existed from 1946 to 1955. For further discussion of this topic, see Head, et al., *Broadcasting*.

1950.[45] Seven Gibson recalled watching wrestling in the 1950s with several friends: "As soon as everybody got TV the wrestling took them over. And I mean, they thought it was real and some still do back home. And those guys, they'd wrestle and I mean they would get mad and one guy in the neighborhood, he shot the TV."[46] This personal interaction with early television was mentioned quite often. As Judy recalled, "It still blows my mind how those people can go through wires or the air. But I knew some people when they would say good night and wave, they'd say good night and wave back, I have seen people do that."[47] Cleland remembered a friend's grandmother and great-aunt:

> They would watch, I don't know what program, but anyway, she wouldn't, the great-aunt would not necessarily be dressed properly and come out into the room with the television on and her sister'd throw a fit. "Get, get back in there," she'd say. "You know they can see ya. If you can see them, they've got to be able to see you [laugh]." They was a lot of people back in the country that had never been exposed to anything like that and they didn't know where it was coming from.[48]

The Novelty Wears Off

Given the economic hardships experienced by many during this period, participants were eager to find diversions and often expressed excitement over this new medium. As Judy recalled, "Hey, all we ever had was a Sears & Roebuck catalog you could take to the outside toilet or listen to the radio and this was wonderful to have a TV and see this and hear this

---

[45] Larry Gianakos, *Television Drama Series Programming: A Comprehensive Chronicle, 1947–1959* (Metuchen NJ: Scarecrow Press, 1980). In the 1980s, wrestling experienced a tremendous growth in popularity when USA Network and Superstation WTBS-Atlanta began coverage of the World Wrestling Federation (WWF) and the (WCW) World Championship Wrestling federation.

[46] Gibson, interview with author.

[47] Bill, interview with author.

[48] Thorpe, interview with author.

right in your living room."[49] However, as more participants in the region got television, fewer spoke of going to visit neighbors, specifically to watch TV. "I know before we got TV we would go to a neighbor's house and watch boxing," remembered Johnnie Rhea. "But people quit visiting when they got their own."[50] In a similar vein, Gould wrote that early television was a boon to bars, as people gathered at their local taverns to watch the new medium. As more people began purchasing their own sets, however, bars began reporting less trade.[51]

According to Lull's examination of the ways in which television facilitated communication, "the medium [television] is used as a convenient resource for entertaining outside guests in the home. To turn on the set when guests arrive is to introduce instant common ground. Strangers in the home may then indulge in 'television talk.'"[52] This was certainly the case when television first arrived in the region. However, with increasing television ownership and the automatic casualness of TV viewing caused by the availability of electricity, many of the positive social aspects of TV viewing disappeared, leading some participants to talk about its negative effects. As Johnnie explained, things changed: "Early on you'd go visit and they'd turn the television on. Later, when you went to visit they'd turn it off. Now, they don't welcome you that much. They leave television on. You don't know whether to go or not, now."[53]

Others, like Linda Lee, believed that television disrupted family unity: "I don't think television brought our family closer together, I think it just kept us focused on something but it didn't help us communicate."[54] Virginia Miller concurred:

[49] Bill, interview with author.

[50] Rhea, interview with author.

[51] Gould, "TV Transforming U.S. Social Scene," 1. Of course, another reason for slower business in bars might have been the inflationary cycle of the early 1950s.

[52] Lull, "The Social Uses of Television," 202.

[53] Rhea, interview with author.

[54] Linda Lee, interview with author, video recording, 19 June 1998, in possession of author.

You don't communicate when you're watching television. You know you may be sitting in the same room, but you have no communication unless you're watching a documentary or something like that. But then you might talk but most of the time you're sitting there just looking at this box and you're not saying a word and half the time one of them has fallen asleep and what point is there, it's just not worth it.[55]

These sentiments were shared by others and were considerably stronger than any negative feelings expressed about radio penetration in the 1930s and 1940s. In fact, rarely did anyone describe radio as disrupting community or family unity. Nevertheless, some defended television as being an educational force. In speaking about the differences between radio and television, Marian Dees said:

TV brought the world in, more so than radio because you could see it. Radio you could hear about it, but with television, you could see. And that made a big difference, made a big impression even on the kids. Anybody that has a television set, if they don't get some kind of education, something's wrong with them. You're supposed to absorb all you can, you know, as you go along, and it helped to do that, it helped to bring the world into you.[56]

Just a Progressive Thing

In many respects, TV followed in the footsteps of radio. Murry and Godfrey found that television's growth greatly benefited from existing radio programming. In addition, they found that radio established the business patterns for television operation, both nationally and locally.[57] Indeed, Clyde Pinney felt the arrival of television had a minimal impact

---

[55] Miller, interview with author.
[56] Dees, interview with author.
[57] Michael Murray and Donald G. Godfrey, eds., *Television in America: Local Station History from across the Nation* (Ames: Iowa State University Press, 1996).

on him compared to how radio's arrival broadened his horizon: "To me, back when radio was going on—when we were listening to the radio—it broadened our horizons so much, from what we had been used to before radio came into existence, that television was just a progressive thing. We just sort of graduated from hearing it to seeing and hearing it at the same time. I don't know if television really made that much impact over radio or not, it was more of a continuation of the radio thing."[58]

Hilmes tells us "television grew directly out of three decades of radio broadcasting, from which it carried over not only its economic, regulatory, and institutional structures but also its familiar program forms, even to specific shows and personalities."[59] Shows that were successful on radio were readily adapted to the new medium. *The Goldbergs, The Life of Riley, Amos 'n' Andy, The Jack Benny Show,* and *I Remember Mama* were just a few of the programs that went from radio to early network television. In fact, more than 200 primetime network television series first aired on network radio.[60] In the case of *Have Gun Will Travel,* the reverse was true. First seen on television in 1957, an audio version of *Have Gun Will Travel* aired on CBS radio from 1958 to 1960.[61] In addition, soap operas quickly made their way from radio to the television screen, although *Guiding Light* was one of the few existing radio serials to make the transition successfully. Broadcast on radio from 1937 to 1956 and on television from 1952 to the present, *Guiding Light* is the longest running serial in broadcasting history.

Realizing that radio stars would likely become television stars, CBS Chairman William Paley devised the radio "talent raids" of 1948–1949. Paley negotiated contracts whereby stars would form corporations naming themselves the major stockholder and asset. CBS would then purchase control of the program from the corporation for a large

---

[58] Clyde Pinney, interview with author.

[59] Michele Hilmes, *Radio Voices: American Broadcasting, 1922–1952* (Minneapolis: University of Minnesota Press, 1997) xiv.

[60] *Ibid.*

[61] I still have my Paladin Colt .45 cap gun. As Paladin described the original: "The balance is excellent, this trigger responds to a pressure of one ounce. This gun was hand crafted to my specifications and I rarely draw it unless I mean to use it."

amount of money. The star would pay tax on capital gains, which was considerably lower than the tax liability on straight income. The plan was so successful that CBS was able to get Freeman Gosden and Charles Correll (stars of *Amos 'n' Andy*), Jack Benny, and Edgar Bergen (*Charlie McCarthy*) from NBC. In addition, Bing Crosby, Red Skelton, and the *Ozzie and Harriet* show also went to CBS. Most of these changes occurred during the 1948–1949 season; however, in the following year, NBC was able to hire Groucho Marx, Bob Hope, Kate Smith, and Ed Wynn away from CBS.[62]

Like many participants I spoke with, Marian Dees, who had been an avid radio listener, followed her favorite radio personality from radio to television:

> There was a woman on the Cincinnati [radio] station, on WLW that had a morning show and I used to listen to it, and got to liking it very much. It was on five days a week and she came on one day and said, "I'm gonna go on television, we're going to be on television." And my husband said, "I know who's going to have a television set before the week's out." And we did! Yeah, I didn't control the money in the house but he tried to make me happy. So, he went out and got me a television.[63]

Although some contend that advertisers abandoned postwar radio for television, Hilmes found that networks deliberately made decisions to concentrate development in the newer medium where sales potential was vast and regulatory conditions favorable. Networks took flourishing postwar radio profits and applied them directly to TV's growth, often at the expense of radio.[64]

In speaking with participants about their favorite radio programs, the *Grand Ole Opry* was mentioned more than any other. Not surprisingly, when the program began broadcasting on television on 15 October 1955, it was also mentioned as one of the most-watched shows.

---

[62] Sterling and Kittross, *Stay Tuned*, 297-301.

[63] Dees, interview with author.

[64] Hilmes, *Radio Voices*, xv.

Frank Frazel remembered, "The first thing that we watched on our television was the *Grand Ole Opry*."[65] Although extremely popular among the participants I spoke to, the *Grand Ole Opry* was originally on network TV (ABC) for less than one year. After its last network broadcast on 15 September 1956, the show went into syndication and was telecast largely in regions where country music was most popular. It was not until 1985 that it again appeared nationally on the Nashville Network.[66]

Another favorite radio program that had a large following among participants I interviewed was *Amos 'n' Andy*. It too became a favorite television program when it was originally broadcast on CBS from 28 June 1951 until 11 June 1953. Westerns (e.g. *Gunsmoke* 1955–1975), comedies (e.g. *I Love Lucy* 1951–1961), and news programs were also mentioned by participants when they were asked to speak about what they were watching when television first came into the region. However, many also mentioned shows that premiered in the 1960s.

Finding Identity on TV

It could be argued that with the introduction of radio, Appalachians in general were by and large "included" with popular shows like the *Grand Ole Opry* and *National Barn Dance*.[67] In fact, some participants even knew performers on the *Grand Ole Opry* and spoke of making sure they tuned-in whenever friends from the "hollow" would perform. Seven Gibson recalled stories about the King of Bluegrass: "One of our pickers and grinners that all of our families would pick and grin with in a little cave beside of my house finally made it to the *Grand Ole Opry*.... The King of Bluegrass, Jimmy Martin."[68] Eliza Collins claims to have given Martin his first guitar lesson: "There was a man from around these parts singing on the *Grand Ole Opry* and we'd sit up til 12:00 til he'd sing. Jimmy Martin, I don't know if you've ever heard tell of him or not. Yeah, I learned him his first three chords on his guitar. We keep in contact. I

---

[65] Frazel, interview with author.

[66] Brooks and Marsh, *The Complete Directory to Prime Time*, 331-32.

[67] See Bill Malone, *Country Music, U.S.A.* (Austin: University of Texas Press, 1985).

[68] Gibson, interview with author.

call sometimes and he comes over and sings for me. We all see him. He was a little ragged boy growin' up.... We'd listen to see if he was alright."[69]

However, in looking at television's early programming, mountain residents were largely excluded. When they were included in CBS's Tuesday night line-up from the 1960s (*The Beverly Hillbillies*, *Green Acres*, and *Hee Haw*), Branscome vehemently criticized the programming as "the most intensive effort ever exerted by a nation to belittle, demean, and otherwise destroy a minority people within its boundaries."[70]

These shows, however, repeatedly came up as programs watched by the participants, who voiced ambivalent and contradictory feelings about the characters. Speaking of the characters on *The Beverly Hillbillies*, Barbara Langdon said: "That's the television's image of mountain people, but they are not what my family is, that's probably why I felt that distance from the images I was seeing and what I experienced in my own family. I mean, I knew that we weren't what we were seeing on TV so that had to be something different."[71] At the same time, some longed to see images on television with whom they could identify and found them in these programs despite the stereotypes. As Tammy Mullins explained: "*The Beverly Hillbillies*, for example, I thought they were great. I mean, because where else were you going to find these people other than around you, you know? 'Cause you really didn't. You always saw the superstars on TV but you never really saw the real people, people that lived around you. So, I really connected with them."[72] Even as participants sought characters on TV with whom to identify, they were mindful that "hillbilly" and rural folks on television were oftentimes depicted in a derogatory manner. These contradictory feelings about identifying with characters on TV, and what I often observed as a palpable desire to be included in the popular culture being presented on

---

[69] Eliza Collins, interview with author.

[70] James Branscome, "Annihilating the Hillbilly: The Appalachians' Struggle with America's Institution," *Katallagete* 3/2 (Winter 1971): 25.

[71] Langdon, interview with author.

[72] Tammy Mullins, interview with author, video recording, 26 June 1999, in possession of author.

television, speaks to the complexity of cultural identity and inclusion.[73] Like Tammy Mullins, Sharon Bolling longed for characters with whom she could identify. Having grown up on Stone Mountain (outside of Wise, Virginia), Sharon spoke of being called a Melungeon in school: "You were called the High Knob Melungeons, you know, just names all the time. Constantly made fun of."[74] It was apparently on *The Andy Griffith Show* that Sharon found people with whom she felt an affinity:

> I loved it. Basically it was just like we was, you know, a little bitty town. You got some on there that's outcasts and some that ain't so.... Maybe Otis. He was always being made fun of and the stuff that he did, he didn't think about. He was always drunk on there.... Otis could have been a Melungeon [laugh]. That would have been a word I would have loved to heard on that show. Even when I was growing up, it would have been nice.[75]

Some lightheartedly embraced the characters on *The Beverly Hillbillies*; however, there still appeared to be some ambivalence. "Well, out my back door lived a hundred of them or so," mused Seven Gibson. "I knew 'em, grew up with 'em, still have a bunch of 'em in my house on Saturday. I knew a hundred Jed Clampetts and then I saw him every day in town, ten or twelve of 'em."[76] But as Judy Bill explained, "I took no offense at it. I thought they were pretty funny myself. I mean, you know, like a lot of people we knew even, like we were even. So, no, I took no offense at it. We just thought it was the way it was."[77]

Connie Mullins Clark's comments about the characters on *The Beverly Hillbillies* perhaps goes to the root of how some Appalachians

---

[73] For further discussion of this issue, see Michael Hogg, Deborah J. Terry, and Katherine M. White, "A Tale of Two Theories: A Critical Comparison of Identity Theory with Social Identity Theory," *Social Psychology Quarterly* 58/4 (December 1995): 255–69.

[74] Sharon Bolling, interview with author, audio recording, 9 July 2004, in possession of author.

[75] *Ibid.*

[76] Gibson, interview with author.

[77] Bill, interview with author.

have internalized the media's view of the stereotypical mountain resident: "Yeah, I remember especially *The Beverly Hillbillies*. We sometimes would laugh at the characters and then other times, we would feel, we wondered if other people thought we were that bad, if other people thought we were that way. If they did, we felt they were seeing a wrong picture of us, that this was very stereotypical of, not all our families are this way."[78]

It is in the statement "not all our families are this way" that Connie appears to accept the media's stereotype for some mountain families. Williamson makes a similar observation about Dolly Parton's comments on the way Hollywood views country and mountain people, and how her fans view Ms Parton. Described by Williamson as "our fullest embodiment of the hillbilly gal as cultural devil," her net worth is estimated at between $100 and $300 million. Quoting Ms Parton, Williamson writes, "The Hollywood version of the country and mountain people has always bothered me. They usually make us a lot more stupid and dumb than we really are."[79] Williamson continues, "The irony in this statement goes to the heart of her greater paradox: in rejecting only the degree (more 'stupid and dumb'), she accepts the basic premise ('stupid and dumb')."[80]

Throughout Appalachia's history, outsiders have come into the region to appropriate its natural resources.[81] What is ironic about *The Beverly Hillbillies*' premise is that the Clampetts achieved their wealth by claiming the mineral rights to the oil discovered on their land. (Apparently, the stereotype of the lazy hillbilly would not permit wealth gained through hard, honest work). This is in contrast to so many

---

[78] Connie Mullins Clark, interview with author, video recording, 26 June 1999, in possession of author.

[79] Jerry Wayne Williamson, *Hillbillyland: What the Movies Did to the Mountains and What the Mountains Did to the Movies* (Chapel Hill: University of North Carolina Press, 1995) 258.

[80] *Ibid.*, 260.

[81] See Harry Caudill, *Night Comes to the Cumberlands, a Biography of a Depressed Area* (Boston: Little, Brown, 1963); Sally Maggard, "Cultural Hegemony: The News Media and Appalachia," *Appalachian Journal* 12/3 (1985): 67-83.

Appalachian families who sold their mineral rights to outside interests.[82] Being too wealthy to remain in the "hills," the Clampetts move to California where, to a certain extent, the roles are reversed. The family becomes "outsiders" while corporate America (e.g. the banker, Mr. Drysdale) becomes the insider. However, the modus operandi remained the same: corporate America continues its attempt to exploit the wealth from the "hillbillies."

Newcomb observes that popular entertainment is dependent on commercial success, and *The Beverly Hillbillies* was one of the most popular television programs of all time. Newcomb suggests that the success of the show is not defined by the fact that the Clampetts are repeatedly being conned, but that viewers of the program (even those from Appalachia) see the mountain folk's rural wisdom and good-hearted nature as morally superior to the opportunists ready to appropriate the family's wealth in nearly every episode. As Newcomb points out: "Invariably, the simpler values of the Clampetts win out over the morally deficient swindlers.... The mountaineer or the hillbilly is being associated with, becomes the metaphor for, a set of more truly American values. These values seem to have disappeared in the sleazy world of Southern California, and the hillbilly's appearance there is a judgment on that world."[83]

As participants discussed their conflicting feelings about characters with whom they identified on television, it appears clear how important electronic media has become in informing these respondents' identity. Even when mindful of the negative depiction of country folk on television, most participants exhibited an unmistakable desire to identify with and be included in the popular culture being presented on television.

As with radio, Appalachians were eager to welcome television into their communities. Just as some people within the region were unable to afford the cost of a radio when they were first marketed, the same was true with television in the 1950s. This resulted in neighborhood

---

[82] See Ronald Eller, *Miners, Millhands, and Mountaineers: Industrialization of the Appalachian South, 1880–1930* (Knoxville: University of Tennessee Press, 1982).

[83] Newcomb, "Appalachia on Television" 159–60.

gatherings at the home of the first TV set in the community. As a result, these initial gatherings appeared to enhance the sense of community within the region.

The arrival of electricity also had a dramatic impact on the ways in which people experienced each medium. Electricity assured that radio could be turned on whenever the listener liked; however, unlike early radios that were battery powered, television had to wait for electricity. The concurrent arrival of television and electricity within the region allowed the television set to become a constant companion more quickly, which was not the case with the arrival of radio. This automatic casualness of TV viewing, along with increasing television ownership, caused many of the positive social aspects of TV viewing to disappear far more rapidly than had occurred during radio's inception. This in turn led some participants to talk about television's negative effect, something that rarely occurred when participants spoke of early radio.

Perhaps more than any other event discussed, participants spoke of the arrival of television into the region with great enthusiasm and remarkable detail. In spite of the obstacles of limited resources, geographical isolation, and cultural stereotypes, rural Appalachians again found ways to join the electronic media revolution.

Chapter Seven

Melungeons and the Internet

In his 1939 study on radio in rural America, Forsyth wrote: "Other sweeping changes may be pending, following from certain technical advances which, it has been suggested, could throw instantaneously the resources of great metropolitan newspapers or national book publishers into the living rooms of every home possessing an instrument which would be not unlike the present radio."[1]

Reading these words more than half a century later, one might think that Forsyth was predicting the advent of the Internet more so than the burgeoning developments in television. In the 1970s, the British, French, and Canadians introduced teletex and videotex devices that would allow news and weather reports, airline schedules, and other text-based information to be transmitted or sent over coaxial or fiber-optic cables to television receivers in homes and businesses. In the United States, the Knight-Ridder newspaper corporation introduced a videotex service in south Florida in 1983 and the Times Mirror Company tried a similar system in Southern California. Both operations closed down within three years. Today, it appears that computers are better suited than television receivers for this type of information retrieval and distribution.[2] Owners of hand-held PC devices are now

---

[1] Howard Forsyth, "The Radio and Rural Research," *Rural Sociology* 4/1 (March 1939): 67.

[2] For a further discussion on this topic, see Sydney Head, Christopher H. Sterling, and Lemuel B. Schofield, *Broadcasting in America: A Survey of Electronic Media* (Boston: Houghton Mifflin, 1994).

able to download newspaper articles, news magazines, and best-selling novels simply by connecting to a phone line or Wi-Fi. In addition, Internet sites, such as bibliomania.com[3] and Project Gutenberg,[4] allow Internet users free access to the entire works of Shakespeare along with a myriad of other books currently in the public domain. As the MCI commercials once assured us, "It's a wonderful time to be alive." One can only wonder how Forsyth would respond.

In the 1960s, Marshall McLuhan predicted that we were at the dawn of a new era of global communications where electronic technology would bring mankind into a "seamless Web of kinship and interdependence."[5] In the 1990s, the rapid expansion of the Internet seemed to suggest that this vision has already been realized. Certainly, in some areas of academic and business research, the Internet has provided an immediate global forum for the access to new information and the exchange and diffusion of ideas. Contemporary mythology, fueled by the rhetoric and vested interests of Internet providers in search of eager consumers, positions the World Wide Web as the most significant phenomenon of the new millennium.[6]

Community and Identity

As stated earlier, while searching for rural Appalachians who had actively embraced the Internet, I found that few of the elderly participants whom I had previously interviewed about radio and television's arrival in Appalachia were Internet users. As I continued my search for an indigenous group within the Appalachian region that had actively embraced the Internet, I became aware that the Melungeon community, through the creation of their own Web sites and listservs, had begun

---

[3] Bibliomania.com, http://bibliomania.com.

[4] Project Gutenberg, http://www.gutenberg.org.

[5] Marshall McLuhan, *Understanding Media: The Extensions of Man* (New York: McGraw-Hill, 1964) 50.

[6] See Janet Lowe, *Bill Gates Speaks: Insight from the World's Greatest Entrepeneur* (New York: John Wiley & Sons, 1998); Bill Gates, *Business @ the Speed of Thought: Using a Digital Nervous System*. With Collins Hemingway. (New York: Warner Books, 1999).

creating their own on-line communities. The establishment of these virtual communities has helped to facilitate annual Melungeon Unions that attract both people living within Melungeon geographic communities and those in diaspora, thereby enlarging the face-to-face community. These processes of Melungeon identity and community building can be illuminated by a number of concepts that have been examined by scholars in the past.

For instance, a number of studies have examined the relationship between the geographical definition of communities and their cultural construction. In looking at analyses of what constitutes community, Wilbur examines the word's etymological origins and finds that it refers "primarily to relations of commonality between person and objects, and only rather imprecisely to the site of such community."[7] In *Imagined Communities*, Anderson[8] examined how a community could be imagined around shared cultural practices, while Deutsch and Foltz[9] have contested the notion of the nation as a geographically-based construction. It might be said that the Melungeons have been self-defined and culturally constructed. On one level, Melungeons historically have been defined geographically. At the same time, Melungeon identity in the past has been culturally constructed by "outsiders" as negative. This negative image was often defensively internalized by insiders through the construction of memory and myths. Today, the use of the Internet has created the opportunity for the Melungeon community to reach out beyond its geographical borders and construct its own identity in a positive way.

Another area of recent scholarship that helps to illuminate the process of Melungeon identity creation is the study of identity and self-

---

[7] Shawn Wilbur, "An Archaeology of Cyberspaces: Virtuality, Community, Identity," in *Internet Culture*, ed. David Porter (New York: Routledge, 1997) 8. Also see *The Oxford English Dictionary*, 2nd ed., s.v. "Community."

[8] Benedict Anderson, *Imagined Communities: Reflections on the Origins and Spread of Nationalism* (New York: Verso, 1983).

[9] Karl Deutsch and William J. Foltz, *Nation-Building* (New York: Atherton Press, 1966).

presentation via the use of computer mediated technology. Dominick[10] and Mitra[11] examine self-presentation on an individual level via Web page production. Dominick writes, "Simply defined, self-presentation refers to the process by which individuals attempt to control the impression others have of them. A personal Web page can be viewed as a carefully constructed self-presentation."[12] Others, like Mohammed[13] and Fürsich and Robins[14] examine the self-representation of groups or countries on the World Wide Web. Perhaps the most obvious concept that could be applied to the Melungeon case, however, is that of the "virtual community." Rheingold describes virtual communities as "social aggregations that emerge from the Net when enough people carry on those public discussions long enough, with sufficient human feeling, to form webs of personal relationships in cyberspace."[15] Jones looks at

---

[10] Joseph Dominick, "Who Do You Think You Are? Personal Home Pages and Self-Presentation on the World Wide Web," *Journalism & Mass Communication Quarterly* 76/4 (December 1999): 646–58.

[11] Ananda Mitra, "Diasporic Websites: Ingroup and Outgroup Discourse," *Critical Studies in Mass Communication* 14/2 (June 1997): 158–81.

[12] Dominick, "Who Do You Think You Are?" 647.

[13] Shaheed Mohammed, "Self-Presentation of Small Developing Countries on the World Wide Web: A Study of Official Websites," *New Media & Society* 6/4 (August 2004): 469–86.

[14] Elfriede Fürsich and Melinda Robins, "Africa.com: The Self-Representation of Sub-Saharan Nations on the World Wide Web," *Critical Studies in Mass Communication* 19/2 (June 2002): 190–211.

[15] Howard Rheingold, *The Virtual Community: Homesteading on the Electronic Frontier* (Reading MA: Addison-Wesley, 1993) 5. Also see Richard Davis, *The Web of Politics: The Internet's Impact on the American Political System* (New York: Oxford University Press, 1999); Brian R. Gaines and Mildred L. G. Shaw, "Human-Computer Interaction in Online Communities," *Journal of Research and Practice in Information Technology* 33/1 (2001): 3–15; Katie Hafner, *The Well: A Story of Love, Death, and Real Life in the Seminal Online Community* (New York: Carroll and Graf, 2001); Kevin A. Hill and John E. Hughes, *Cyberpolitics: Citizen Activism in the Age of the Internet* (Lanham MD: Rowman & Littlefield, 1998); David Holmes, ed., *Virtual Politics: Identity and Community in Cyberspace* (London: Sage, 1997); Amy Jo Kim, *Community Building on the Web* (Berkeley CA: Peachpit Press, 2000); Pippa Norris, *Digital Divide: Civic Engagement, Information, Poverty, and the Internet Worldwide* (Cambridge: Cambridge University Press, 2001); Jenny Preece, "Sociability and Usability in Online Communities: Determining and Measuring Success," *Behaviour*

relationships between individuals and virtual communities, arguing that electronic virtual communities are places where "individuals shape their own community by choosing which other communities to belong to.... [We] will be able to forge our own places from among the many that exist, not by creating new places but by simply choosing from the menu of those available."[16] However, within the Melungeon community, members are not simply "choosing which other communities to belong to," they are in fact creating their own Web sites and listservs that help further redefine their identity more positively than past historical representations. Computer-mediated technology has enabled Melungeons to establish a virtual community larger than the original geographic community through its inclusion of members from a common location (e.g. Sneedville, Tennessee, and Wise, Virginia), in addition to members living in diaspora.

Indeed, many scholars have examined the impact technology has had on issues of communication. Some, like Postman[17] and Pacey,[18] have been somewhat dubious about any positive influence technology has had on society, while others view the use of technology as an augmentation to the communication process.[19] According to Baym, "the dominant concern underlying most criticism of on-line community is that in an increasingly fragmented off-line world, on-line groups substitute for "real" (i.e., geographically local) community, falling short in several interwoven regards."[20] In looking at virtual communities, Sherry Turkle

---

and *Information Technology* 20/5 (2001): 347–56; Howard Rheingold, *Smart Mobs: The Next Social Revolution* (Cambridge MA: Perseus, 2002).

[16] Steven Jones, "Understanding Community in the Information Age," in *Cybersociety 2.0: Computer-Mediated Communication and Community*, ed. Steven Jones (Thousand Oaks CA: Sage Publications, 1995) 11.

[17] Neil Postman, *Technopoly: The Surrender of Culture to Technology* (New York: Vintage Books, 1993).

[18] Arnold Pacey, *The Culture of Technology* (Cambridge MA: The MIT Press, 1994).

[19] For example, see Bill Gates, *The Road Ahead*, (New York: Viking, 1996); Nicholas Negroponte, *Being Digital* (New York: Alfred Knopf, 1995).

[20] Nancy Baym, "The Emergence of On-Line Community," in *Cybersociety 2.0: Computer-Mediated Communication and Community*, ed. Steven Jones (Thousand Oaks CA: Sage Publications, 1995) 36. Also see David Silver, "Selling Cyberspace:

states that "virtual experience may be so compelling that we believe that within it we've achieved more than we have."[21] However, it appears that a large number of Melungeons who initially met one another via the Internet took their cyber-friendship experience to the next level by actually meeting one another at the Unions, thereby creating a unique face-to-face community that combines elements of their geographical and virtual communities.

In *The Roots of Modern Media Analysis*, Carey describes early communication technology as promising the distribution of information everywhere, "simultaneously reducing the economic advantage of the city and bringing the more varied urban culture out to the countryside."[22] Because of their geographical isolation, Melungeons living in rural communities appear to have much to gain from computer mediated communication, especially given its ability to decrease the significance of spatial distance dramatically. In *Communication as Culture*, Carey also states, "Communication under a ritual view is the sacred ceremony that draws persons together in fellowship and commonality."[23] As Melungeons began to reach out to one another in hopes of forming community via electronic communications technology, some of their practices reflect Carey's ritual view of communication. At the same time, their use of the Internet has allowed many to trace their genealogy and form communities, both virtually and geographically. What follows are some of their oral history stories.

Constructing and Deconstructing the Rhetoric of Community," *Southern Communication Journal* 70/3 (Spring 2005): 187–99; Beth Kolko and Elizabeth Reid, "Dissolution and Fragmentation: Problems in Online Communities," in *Cybersociety 2.0: Computer-Mediated Communication and Community*, ed. Steven Jones (Thousand Oaks CA: Sage Publications, 1995).

[21] Sherry Turkle, "Virtuality and its Discontents," *The American Prospect* 7/24 (Winter 1996): 53.

[22] James Carey, "The Roots of Modern Media Analysis," in *James Carey: A Critical Reader*, ed. Eve Stryker Munson and Catherine A. Warren (Minneapolis: University of Minnesota Press, 1997) 45.

[23] James Carey, *Communication as Culture: Essays on Media and Society* (Boston: Unwin Hyman, 1989) 7.

Finding Identity on the Net

Individual Identity. Many Melungeons have found a new way to reconfigure the past and reconstruct their identity through genealogical research, which, as a result, introduced them to the Internet. Tracking genealogical information on her grandmother, Nancy Sparks Morrison, originally from Charleston, West Virginia (more than 200 miles northeast of Sneedville, Tennessee), spoke of getting on the Net:

> I got a computer [in 1997] and started putting my genealogy into it. And I got on the Internet, and I put a note on one of the [genealogy] message boards saying I'm looking for this Indian grandmother, her name is Mary Collins. And I got a reply from a girl who lived in California and she said your Collins is in the area of the Melungeons, in the area where the Melungeons were. And I wrote her back and said, "Who the heck are Melungeons?" So she gave me a little brief thing, I went to the library and I found Brent [Kennedy]'s book and I sat down and read the book and it just clicked. I knew immediately that this was where this family belonged, was in this character. So, I began doing more research. I have about seven lines that I think are Melungeon connected.... I don't think I would have found it without the Internet.[24]

Barbara Langdon, originally from Lincoln, Nebraska, tells a similar story of finding a Melungeon family connection on the Net:

> Well, when I first started doing research, the first thing I did was get on the Internet. There are several genealogy sites [where] you can post your names you are looking for and dates and regions and all that sort of thing, and I had posted information on my grandfather's family and within just a couple weeks I had contacts from distant cousins.... A cousin I've never met told me this family story about how we were Melungeon,

---

[24] Nancy Sparks Morrison, interview with author, audio recording, 18 June 2004, in possession of author.

and the way he told his story, and the way that his family reacted to being Melungeon was very, very similar to my own experience with being told that we were Indian and the sort of barrier there about, you know.[25]

Having grown up in diaspora, neither of these women was ever told of their Melungeon ancestry as children, yet each credits the Internet with helping them find a part of their heritage. Some participants who found a Melungeon connection on the Net spoke of their families' acceptance (however reluctant) of Native American ancestry while avoiding any mention of African or Melungeon heritage. In fact, seldom would participants even recall hearing the word Melungeon in connection with their families' ancestry.

However, like Nancy and Barbara, many participants I interviewed appeared to be ready to embrace their identity. This is especially poignant given the history of discrimination many Melungeons faced over the years. However, there still appeared to be a great deal of soul-searching among the participants with whom I spoke. As Barbara put it, "I think right now my question that I am trying to answer is, how do we define Melungeon? And, in some ways it's, you know, it is a self-identifying, uh, let's see, how do I want to say that? Uh, in a lot of ways, people that are Melungeon are self-identified."[26] Fitzgerald tells us: "By defining itself, ethnically or otherwise, a group escapes classification by others."[27] Perhaps this is the objective of the self-representation towards which the Melungeon community is headed.

Construction of a Virtual Community. Today, a simple Google search of the word Melungeon produces over 97,000 hits. Back in the mid 1990s, while a graduate assistant at the University of Kentucky, Darlene Wilson started one of the first Melungeon Web sites. Her intention was to create "a free space for all different ideas, all different theories…that was the potential that I think I saw at the beginning, and many people

---

[25] Langdon, interview with author.

[26] *Ibid.*

[27] Thomas Fitzgerald, "Media and Changing Metaphors of Ethnicity and Identity," *Media, Culture & Society* 13/2 (April 1991): 202.

saw at the beginning...an opportunity to begin to push over those barriers to trans-ethnic, multi-ethnic understanding."[28] As people began to use the computer for genealogical research, the Internet became an invaluable tool. "The computer/Internet made it so much easier to do genealogy," Darlene continued. "People began to define family groups, family communities. That's still probably more resilient than larger trans-ethnic or trans-family groups like the Melungeons... I think the Internet coincided with the inexpensive PC and a...exponential growth and opportunity for genealogical research. Okay.... Without those three things in combination, there would not have been a Melungeon movement."[29]

For many, Melungeon Web sites became locations where those interested in their heritage, especially those living in diaspora, could find information not easily available elsewhere. Tammy Mullins, whose father was originally from Sneedville, Tennessee, grew up outside of Knoxville, in Jefferson City, Tennessee:

> I always knew that I was from someplace else because I was always looked at a little different in my county because of my hair and my skin type and things like that.... Well, I have very curly hair and dark skin and the eyes. I've also recently, through the Web page, found out about the bump in the back of the head and the shovel teeth[30] thing and I've got all of that and I'm like, this is just really weird because, you know, in school I felt like I was the only one, you know, because everybody else was like "Hey, where are you from?" because I looked so different. I felt alienated, really stood out from my Mom...she would hate to go

---

[28] Darlene Wilson, interview with author, audio recording, 18 June 2004, in possession of author.

[29] *Ibid.*

[30] In addition to dark skin and hair, other characteristics generally accepted as identifying markers of people of Melungeon heritage are a pronounced bump on the back of the head and front teeth with a shovel-shaped inner surface.

to town with me in the summertime. I was really dark. She was really embarrassed.[31]

In addition, Melungeon Web sites proved important in getting participants involved in a virtual community. As Connie Mullins Clark recalled:

> About six months after I got my computer [in 1997], this article in the paper was explaining about a picnic about Melungeon heritage. People could send in, over the Internet, they could fill out the form, send it in, and you could be part of the picnic. So, I did that. I went directly to the Web, you know, hooked on the Web site, went in there, filled out my application, printed it off and sent it. So, I have been, since that time, I have worked directly with the Internet, helping with Web pages and working on research with Melungeons.... There's different Web sites now that you can go to and find the Melungeon information, but that's how I first got started with Melungeons. I had it [a computer], but to really get involved in the Internet itself was with the Melungeon connection.[32]

One way some people participated in community building was though developing common and inclusive rituals, which Carey describes as being "directed not toward the extension of messages in space but toward the maintenance of society in time; not the act of imparting information but the representation of shared beliefs.... Under a ritual view, then, news is not information but drama."[33] In joining the Melungeon listserv, I was surprised by the large number of e-mails I would receive each day. Often, the same individual would post ten to twenty messages within a twenty-four hour period, and the content seemed to become less important than the ritual of posting messages. At times, the information conveyed via the unmonitored listserv was merely

---

[31] Mullins, interview with author.
[32] Clark, interview with author.
[33] Carey, *Communication as Culture*, 18–21.

chitchat. For instance, over the course of one week, there were hundreds of messages discussing whether a type of heat rash was indicative of Melungeon heritage.

Madonna Cook, who was already aware of her Melungeon identity, used the Web sites and Melungeon listserv to research her legacy: "I already knew of the Melungeon connection for my family when I went on-line so I started looking for other people who were researching these same lines to see if they had something that I didn't have. [I use] the Melungeon list, which has automatic e-mails coming to you, where they have a lot of discussion about the Melungeons. I was getting like 300 e-mails a day off that one list."[34] To those tracing their lineage, the number of postings could be overwhelming. Barbara spoke of trying to keep up:

> Just to keep up with what's happening with the Melungeon research, you know, at first, I was using the Internet, oh gosh, I was on there hours, you know, listening to everybody tell their stories. There are a lot of stories on that listserv. People telling their stories about, you know, why they think they are Melungeon or why they got interested in the Melungeons because of, you know, some story in the family, or they always knew, or they have a history of Black Dutch.[35]

As Melungeons began to reach out to one another on the Net, their multiple postings of messages on the listserv appeared to be in many ways a ritual that drew "persons together in fellowship and commonality."[36]

Coming "Face-to-Face"

Many have pointed to the Internet as the main catalyst for bringing so many members of the Melungeon community together for their first annual face-to-face meeting in 1997. Originally planned as a picnic for

---

[34] Cook, interview with author.
[35] Langdon, interview with author.
[36] Carey, *Communication as Culture*, 7.

50–60 people, First Union was attended by approximately one thousand people, many of whom expressed an interest in learning more about their heritage. Most attribute the large attendance to the Internet's broad reach. As Darlene recalls, "I will never forget the first show (First Union), when we were expecting a picnic of 60 people and close to 1,000 showed up. It was all by e-mail...it was all by Internet."[37] Cleland Thorpe spoke of meeting others at the Unions from outside of the Appalachia region: "I talked to people in California and I then talked to people in Arkansas and Tennessee, up in Ohio and it was just, you know, it's really weird how we all have so much in common, and it really had to come from our heritage. I mean, it passed on, it had to be."[38] Had it not been for the simultaneous postings on the Net, it would have been unlikely that people Cleland met from California, Arkansas, and Ohio would have had access to the local newspaper article that announced the First Union.

The bonds made in cyberspace seemed to create a bond similar to that of a real family that was reinforced when participants met at the Unions. As Nancy put it, "It amazed me, the emotional feeling that I got. It was just like we were coming to a family reunion."[39]

Is It Real or Is It Virtual?

Turkle[40] addresses the issue that in certain situations, virtual communities can, for some, become a substitute for the real world.[41] However, a large number of Melungeons who initially met one another via the Internet took their cyber-friendship experience to the next level by making a point of meeting one another at the Unions. In fact, many participants mentioned how nice it was to make human contact with people with whom they had created an electronic community. Nancy

---

[37] Wilson, interview with author.

[38] Thorpe, interview with author.

[39] Morrison, interview with author.

[40] Turkle, "Virtuality and its Discontents," 53.

[41] For a discussion of how the Internet is neither a "place-less space" nor a "place separate from the real world," see Daniel Miller and Don Slater, *The Internet: An Ethnographic Approach* (Oxford: Berg, 2000).

admits: "It's interesting because I never really felt that I belonged. I've always been kind of a private person.... I never felt really comfortable in this group or that group or the other group. It was just not—and when I found the Melungeons and the first time I went to Wise, Virginia, [where the First Union was held] I felt like I was coming home. It amazed me, the emotional feeling that I got."[42] Claude Collins had similar feelings: "It was more interesting Saturday up at Berea [at the Melungeon genealogical workshop] when I could look people in the eye and hear them talk. I was standing there Saturday in one of these meetings and this lady come runnin' up and she threw her arms around my neck and she said 'Oh, I'm so glad to see what you look like', 'cause she had e-mailed me dozens and dozens and dozens of times."[43]

So, it appears that for many Melungeon virtual community members, the establishment of a face-to-face community was an important evolution of their on-line experience. As Wayne Winkler explained: "It was a real virtual community and one that really made itself more of a real physical community by creating First Union and then the subsequent Unions. These people who had met only on-line wanted to meet in person. And they wanted to just get to know each other as real people so a...a...the Internet, I think, is really the thing that brought all this together starting in about 1997—1998...right along in there."[44]

As with any first meeting, for some participants, like Barbara, there still was a bit of apprehension:

> It was sort of strange coming to Wise the first time and not having met these people, but having created a community, an electronic community, I'd had experiences before with having a community and bringing that community together through electronic media, through the Internet. And so I was sort of

---

[42] Morrison, interview with author.

[43] Claude Collins, interview with author, audio recording, 28 June 1999, in possession of author.

[44] Wayne Winkler, interview with author, audio recording, 17 June 2004, in possession of author.

nervous about what was going to happen since all of us had met on the Internet and had not met each other yet, because people that I didn't even know were paying attention to what I was saying, you know. "Oh Barb, I've been listening, you know I've been reading what you've been saying on the Internet and I'm so happy to meet you and what do you think about...." You know, it was strange in a very pleasant sort of way, but, it, I didn't know what to expect, I was a little apprehensive and I wondered if I was nuts and what am I doing going to meet all of these people from the Internet. Yeah.[45]

The phrase, "What am I doing going to meet all of these people from the Internet," suggests that the Internet is an actual place in space rather than an electronic medium. Addressing the metaphor of a digital world, Sproull and Faraj tell us, "When e-mail is used for group conversations, the network takes on the characteristics of place—like the office coffee pot or the local watering hole."[46] In fact, the bonds made in cyberspace by most participants I spoke to appeared to last. When speaking of people she has met on the Internet, Barbara admits, "I keep checking the [Melungeon] Web pages to see what's going on and I keep in contact with, there's key people, there's some people that I have long-lasting relationships with now through the Internet that I stay in touch with."[47]

In addition to meeting cyber-friends at Unions, some, like Nancy, spoke of how she gets together with virtual community friends whenever they pass through the region: "I have had some people who were traveling who came by my house and stopped in the area and we had luncheon and visited. They were doing genealogy research. Going to visit family.... We go to dinner and lunch here and talk and meet. So it's

---

[45] Langdon, interview with author.

[46] Lee Sproull and Samer Faraj, "Some Consequences of Electronic Groups," in *Internet Dreams: Archetypes, Myths, and Metaphors*, ed. Mark Stefik (Cambridge: MIT Press, 1996) 134. Also see, Jones, "Understanding Community," 10-35.

[47] Langdon, interview with author.

the Internet. The friendship started on the Internet then continues here or as people are coming through."[48]

So it appears that, even for those living in diaspora, the Internet has enabled individuals interested in Melungeon heritage easy access to the virtual and face-to-face communities. For participants like Tammy Mullins, whose father grew up in Sneedville, but who currently lives outside of counties with a notable Melungeon presence, the Net brought information about the Melungeon community she might not have found elsewhere. As Tammy explained, "I feel like the Internet has really opened up the world to everyone. And also, it's really opened up the world for Melungeon people because, basically, without the Internet and there are very few books that are written, I mean, where would you be? You wouldn't know where to start so actually, the Internet really opened up a big space for me to be able to do research."[49]

The Internet as Electronic Front Porch

Writing about technology's ability to bring strangers together, Johnson compared the computer to the cotton gin, which caused millions of workers at the end of the eighteenth century to crowd together in factory towns. By the early 1800s, Luddites, protesting the drudgery and deskilling brought about by this new labor-saving textile machinery, reacted by smashing the gins.[50] Neo-Luddites might have similar feelings toward the computer and the Internet. Even if most people are not so threatened as to feel a need to toss their computers out the window, for some there is still an enigmatic quality to the computer. On a recent trip on US Airways, both outgoing and incoming flights were delayed by over an hour because of improper luggage distribution in the cargo hold. Each time this happened, the pilot readily blamed the computer for causing the improper distribution, as if it were the computer and not the luggage handlers that overloaded the cargo bay. "Please bear with us," pleaded the pilot, "as we try to get the bugs out of

---

[48] Morrison, interview with author.

[49] Mullins, interview with author.

[50] Steven Johnson, *Interface Culture: How New Technology Transforms the Way We Create and Communicate* (San Francisco: Harper Edge, 1997).

our new computer system." It appeared that the pilot was demonizing the computer.

Similarly, as previously mentioned by some elderly participants, the rapid expansion of the Internet appeared to produce an undercurrent of frustration. This may be in response to people's discomfort with new technology versus personal human interaction. However, as with radio and television's arrival in rural Appalachia, the Internet enhanced community interaction. In addition to the Melungeon cyber-communities, which resulted in face-to-face Unions, some participants spoke of how using the Net, even at home alone, allowed one to interact with others in chat rooms. Some compared their experiences on the Net with a time when one sat on the front porch and chatted with passing neighbors. Bob Cole explains his point of view:

> I think that between TV and air conditioning, people retreat to their homes and tend to isolate themselves inside of the house whereas radio brought you to the porch in the summertime, and the neighbors walked along the street and then the neighbors would stop and listen to the radio and then they'd discuss the news or listen to the programs. So there was a lot of interaction of people and everybody knew everything that was going on in the neighborhood. The Internet, I think, is a technological innovation that tends maybe to counteract the seclusion that was caused by the air conditioning. Well, you start talking to people again. Start communicating with people. You're able to meet people. It's kind of like sittin' on the porch and the neighbors walking up and down the street. You know, they come in, they get in contact. Well, you sit in your house but you get out on the Internet and it's like a stream of people walking by. You can reach out and interrelate with them like you used to when you sat on the front porch and the neighbors walked up and down the street.[51]

---

[51] Cole, interview with author.

The Melungeon use of the Internet and this idea of "electronic front porch" seem to point to a more egalitarian and accessible electronic public sphere. In *The Public Sphere*, Habermas views democracy as representing a social space wherein members of the society can rationally debate issues. The Habermasian view of the public sphere was inspired by the literary movement and revealed itself in salons and coffeehouses where the average citizen could discuss socio-political issues. Although the bourgeois public sphere was marked by gender and class exclusion, Habermas's ideal public sphere was egalitarian in principle.[52] This concept of the public sphere illuminates Internet usage in Appalachia. On the Melungeon listserv issues of gender, age, and race need not have impact on the topic being discussed (if the writer chooses not to reveal his or her physical identity). Newsgroups and listservs offer any subscriber a chance to express his or her ideas without prejudice arising from anything other than what is written.[53] However, a person with a lower educational level might be betrayed by improper use of spelling and grammar. As a result, this person might be taken less seriously in virtual groups. Again, technology, such as automatic grammar and spell-checking software, can level the playing field, leading to a more egalitarian and accessible electronic public sphere.

However, the issue of the "digital divide" remains especially noticeable within rural Appalachia (along with other rural areas of the country). Many poor rural people do not have Internet access. As with other obstacles, participants without local Internet access found ways of connecting, though, often at a premium. "I have the Internet now," says Bennie Lawson. "In the beginning, the only way I could get the Internet was to pay $20 for unlimited access to a [larger city] phone line and then

---

[52] Jurgen Habermas, "The Public Sphere," in *Jurgen Habermas On Society and Politics: A Reader*, ed. Steven Seidman (Boston: Beacon Press, 1989) 231–36.

[53] For further discussion on how textual communication on the Net can minimize traditional identity cues, see Holmes, *Virtual Politics*; Katelyn McKenna and John A. Bargh, "Coming out in the Age of the Internet: Identity 'Demarginalization' through Virtual Group Participation," *Journal of Personality and Social Psychology* 75/3 (September 1998): 681–94; David Silver, "Margins in the Wires: Looking for Race, Gender, and Sexuality in the Blacksburg Electronic Village," in *Race in Cyberspace*, ed. Beth E. Kolko, et al. (New York: Routledge, 2000) 133–50.

I had to pay $25 for an Internet provider service, so it was $45 a month to get [dial-up] Internet access."[54] Madonna told an Internet access story that recalled telephone party lines[55] of the 1930s, 1940s, and 1950s:

> It's a toll call and I knew better than to get on the Internet and there'd be a $6 an hour charge—the way we wanted to research, it takes a long time sometimes to find just what you're looking for. There was access to—there was a lady who had set it up as a non-profit thing where you could share an Internet access line but ten or twelve people had to share. I checked into that but I really didn't want to do that because I figured if we got on there and researched we'd probably take up too much time.[56]

In addition, the up-front cost of getting on-line (hardware, software, and access expenses) was prohibitive for some with fixed or lower incomes. As Marian Dees put it, "It may be cheaper to send an e-mail but the initial cost wasn't cheap. Sooner or later you're gonna spend your money on something."[57]

Just as access to electricity seemed to have determined how people listened to early radio, limited local Internet access in rural Appalachia inhibited some participants' use of the Net. Nevertheless, as with other electronic media, many participants I spoke with were eager to embrace the World Wide Web.

Despite the obstacles to Internet use in Appalachia, the World Wide Web has allowed many participants to connect to one another and to the world at large. It has also allowed the Melungeon population, including those living in diaspora, to redefine their individual identities, to re-envision their community as being more numerous than they had originally imagined, and to define themselves less as a geographic

---

[54] Lawson, interview with author.

[55] Interestingly, the telephone party-line provided a social outlet similar to some Internet chat lines. For further discussion on this topic, see Pavel Curtis, "Mudding: Social Phenomena in Text-Based Virtual Realities," in *Internet Dreams: Archetypes, Myths, and Metaphors*, ed. Mark Stefik (Cambridge: MIT Press, 1996) 265–92.

[56] Cook, interview with author.

[57] Dees, interview with author.

community than as an electronic community. In addition, unlike some virtual communities that may become substitutes for real geographical communities, Melungeon Net users often expanded their on-line experiences to include face-to-face relationships. Thus we see that the Internet can be used as a powerful tool to unify even the most isolated and dispersed groups. Its potential as a public forum is especially powerful in a region where getting to a town meeting could require traversing mountainous terrain or traveling great distances, as is the case in much of Appalachia.

It may be too soon for participants to gauge accurately the Internet's immediate impact on their lives given that this new medium is evolving on almost a daily basis. The Melungeon case demonstrates that further research in other rural and/or dispersed communities throughout the world will show the Net's potential for becoming a unifying, perhaps even egalitarian tool.

Chapter Eight

Conclusion

I am a child of television. I grew up with little Ricky on the *I Love Lucy* television program. Rather than rushing home from school to listen to *Jack Armstrong—The All-American Boy*, I rushed home to watch re-runs of *Gilligan's Island*. I developed my love for cooking while watching Graham Kerr's *The Galloping Gourmet* and Julia Child's *The French Chef*. Television was, among other things, my babysitter, my teacher, and my travel guide. I love TV! I also love the Internet. I guess it would be safe to say that I love electronic media technology. Throughout my life, there has always been a flickering TV screen in the corner of the living room. In the future, as people look back on their youth, many may say the same thing about that computer monitor in the den. If the past is any indication, however, people will always get together to watch (or listen to) the big game or championship fight. But will they gather to watch on a giant plasma-screen hung over the fireplace or on individual two-inch cell phone screens?

In the 1960s, Marshall McLuhan predicted that we were at the dawn of a new era of global communications. In 1999, on the eve of the new millennium, demonstrators gathered in Seattle, Washington, to protest the World Trade Organization. Some of their concerns were that the global marketplace appears to be driving much of our nation's economic and political policies. It is incumbent upon "the people" to be ever mindful of the power of electronic media technology. The Internet is not just another marketing tool for multinational conglomerates attempting to ply their wares and gather information on unwary Web users. Our government developed the Net and it is the people's.

As demonstrated by the Melungeon community, the Internet can be used as a powerful tool to unify even the most isolated groups. In *Technology and Ideology: The Case of the Telegraph*, Carey observed how the telegraph was arguably the first technology that effectively separated communication from transportation.[1] Today, the ability of the Internet and electronic communications technology to shrink the time it takes to move messages over space decreases the significance of spatial distance as a constraint. This could be especially beneficial to Appalachia, given the region's geographical isolation and mountainous terrain. In the 1960s and 1970s, even the poorest homes within Appalachia were likely to have had television antennae protruding from their rooftops. Today, the same might be said for satellite dishes, which help bring signals into the most remote "hollers." Because of their geographical isolation, rural communities have so much to gain from new technologies.

In the past, affordable video equipment made it possible for grassroots activists to document issues often ignored by corporate-controlled media. Nonetheless, the problem of distribution remains since access to channels of communication continues to be controlled by mainstream media. The Internet, however, has the potential to provide a readily accessible public forum for topics concerning groups that were neglected in the past.

In thinking about the future of media and technology in this age of global media conglomeration, let us look at the current structure of radio in context of its arrival in rural Appalachia. During the 1920s and 1930s, radio had a profound effect on rural Appalachian communities. Contrary to the "lonely crowd" theory, where electronic media were sometimes looked upon as isolating forces on society, the inception of radio in Appalachia appeared to enhance rather than disrupt family and community cohesion. In addition to getting out of the house to attend church on Sundays and prayer meetings on Wednesday nights, going to a friend's or neighbor's house on Saturday night to listen to the *Grand*

---

[1] Carey, "Technology and Ideology", 303-306.

Ole Opry on the radio became a big event in the lives of many participants who were interviewed. Moreover, the ability of residents to identify strongly with regional country music programs such as WNOX's *Midday Merry-Go-Round* broadcast from Knoxville, Tennessee, emphasizes the importance of local radio programming.

Today, high-powered commercial radio stations broadcast to broadly defined audiences. For instance, with Clear Channel Communications, homogenized programming decisions made in San Antonio, Texas, are disseminated to over 1,200 stations across the United States. In addition, Clear Channel's Premier Radio Network syndicates more than 100 programs to more than 7,800 radio stations and has equity interests in over 240 radio stations internationally.[2] In 2000, the Federal Communication Commission began to license low-power FM radio stations (LPFM) to serve individual community needs. However, existing broadcasters successfully lobbied congress to limit dramatically the number of low-power stations. As a result, instead of the thousands of LPFM stations in the United States, there are just hundreds.[3]

Elsewhere in the world, however, there are countless low-power stations targeted to specifically defined communities. In Paris, France, alone, nearly one forth of all FM frequencies are assigned to "community stations." Among these "radio associatives" are an anarchist station; a station closely associated with the right-wing National Front; Jewish, Protestant, and Catholic stations; a station with programming for gay listeners; along with stations that target minority listeners, including North African, Flemish, Basque, Bosnian, Kurdish, and Portuguese.[4]

---

[2] Clear Channel Communications, http://www.clearchannel.com/.

[3] David Croteau and William Hoynes, *Media Society: Industries, Images, and Audiences*, 3rd ed. (Thousand Oaks: Pine Forge Press, 2003). On 19 February 2004, the FCC submitted its "Report to the Congress on the Low Power FM Interference Testing Program" in which it recommended "the modification or elimination of minimum distance separation requirements for low power FM ("LPFM") stations" (http://hraunfoss.fcc.gov/edocs_public/attachmatch/DOC-244128A1.pdf). If approved, this recommendation would relax some restrictions on the licensing of LPFM stations. Today, there are approximately 700 LPFM stations in the US.

[4] Mark Poindexter, "Radio in Paris: Can Community Stations Survive?" *Journal*

Low-power radio stations also serve a valuable role in the dissemination of social information in areas of the world with low literacy levels, limited financial resources, and developing areas without electricity.[5]

Perhaps it is again time to revisit how effectively low-power stations can serve small communities' needs, which are often overlooked within the "McDonaldization" of media today. Certainly, within all developing areas of the globe, low-power radio, with its lower costs, can provide much needed information on health, agriculture, and education. Throughout the world, low-power stations can provide specific communities of local interest with a means for information exchange and identity building.

With the advancement of cellular telephone technology, many underdeveloped areas of the world are now better able to take advantage of telephone access, which may not have been as readily available if traditional wiring of the region was required. This could make possible the widespread use of Web radio, which could perform the function of old style clear channel stations, linking people nationally and even internationally, but avoiding the homogenization methods of multinational conglomerations like Clear Channel Communications. Web radio could bring news and entertainment into underprivileged regions of the world not already within the receiving area of traditional broadcast stations. Just as the arrival of radio into rural Appalachia addressed individual communities, the arrival of Web radio could result in the increase of communal listening habits in underdeveloped regions without radio stations. Residents could gather at community centers, or even listen to the news while riding on a bus, thereby creating an opportunity whereby issues of the day could be discussed with other members of the community. Of course, Web radio could also

of Radio Studies 4 (1997): 253–68.
    [5] See Anthony A. Olorunnisola, "Radio and African Rural Communities: Structural Strategies for Social Mobilization," _Journal of Radio Studies_ 4 (1997): 242–52; Rick Rockwell, "Finding Power of Hidden Radio Audiences in the Fields of Guatemala," _Journal of Radio Studies_ 8/2 (Winter 2001): 425–41.

complement areas with established broadcast stations by bringing alternative voices into a region.[6]

The rapid expansion of electronic communication technology seems to suggest that McLuhan's vision of a new era of global communications has been realized. Nonetheless, as we catapult into the next millennium, digitally powered by the computer, it is important to look back in history at how earlier media helped pave the way to the information super-highway.

---

[6] Jacob J. Podber, "The Debut of Broadcasting in Small Town America: A Reflection of Community Radio throughout the World." *Global Media Journal* 3/4 (Spring 2004), http://lass.calumet.purdue.edu/cca/gmj/sp04/gmj-sp04-podber.htm.

Appendix A

Interviews

Armstrong, Georgia, b. 1949. Adams County, Ohio.
Bill, Judy, b. 1940. Strawberry Plains, Tennessee.
Bolling, Sharon, b. 1965. Stone Mountain, Wise County, Virginia.
Boring, Rhea, b. 1926. Vinton County, Ohio.
Borne, Pearl, b. 1907. Vinton County, Ohio.
Clark, Connie Mullins, b. 1948. Wise County, Virginia.
Cole, Bob, b. 1937. Raleigh, North Carolina.
Colley, Florence, b. 1915. Franklin County, Ohio.
Collins, Claude, b. 1927. Sneedville, Tennessee.
Collins, Eliza, b. 1920. Newman's Ridge, Hancock County, Tennessee.
Collins, Pearlie, b. 1904. Rose Hill, Virginia.
Cook, Madonna, b. 1946. Wise County, Virginia.
Cross, Roy. Athens County, Ohio (Telephone interview).
Daugherty, Bernice, b. 1922. Meigs County, Ohio.
Davidson, David, b. 1956. Knoxville, Tennessee.
Dees, Marian, b. 1912. Lebanon, Pennsylvania.
Dobbins, Betty, b. 1930. Meigs County, Ohio.
Edwards, Maude, b. 1897. Wise County, Virginia.
Ellis, Sam, b. 1925. Bell County, Kentucky.
Faught, Helen, b. 1917. Vinton County, Ohio.
Faught, Langley, b. 1919. Vinton County, Ohio.
Flowers, Irene, b. 1935. Athens County, Ohio.
Frazel, Frank, b. 1922. Franklin County, Ohio.
Frezel, Evelyn, b. 1928. Franklin County, Ohio.
Gibson, Bulldog, b. 1940. Newman's Ridge, Hancock County, Tennessee.

Gibson, Seven, b. 1946. Newman's Ridge, Hancock County, Tennessee.

Goins, Phil, b. 1967. Whitley County, Kentucky.

Greer, Archie. Athens County, Ohio (Telephone interview).

Grim, Francis, b. 1914. Meigs County, Ohio.

Grim, Sam, b. 1954. Meigs County, Ohio.

Hart, Golda, b. 1919. Vinton County, Ohio.

Hill, Veva, b. 1975. Meigs County, Ohio.

Hopkins, Sam, b. 1919. Hancock County, Tennessee.

Horrocks, Mary, b. 1915. Geauga County, Ohio.

Hudson, Alexandra, b. 1959. Knott County, Kentucky.

Irwin, Edith, b. 1933. Vinton County, Ohio.

Johnson, Mattie Ruth, b. 1940. Newman's Ridge, Hancock County, Tennessee.

Kennedy, N. Brent. Kingsport, Tennessee.

Langdon, Barbara Tracy, b. 1958. Omaha, Nebraska.

Lawson, Bennie Coffey, b. 1934. Cairo, Oklahoma.

Lee, Linda, b. 1945. Vinton County, Ohio.

Marsh, Bridget, b. 1950. Iberville Parish, Louisiana.

McWhorton, Ruth, b. 1925. Guernsey County, Ohio.

Miller, Virginia, b. 1946. Marion County, Ohio.

Morrison, Ken, b. 1910. Athens County, Ohio.

Morrison, Nancy Sparks, b. 1938. Charleston, West Virginia.

Mullins, Tammy, b. 1950. Jefferson City, Tennessee.

Nalley, Patrick, b. 1929. Louisville, Kentucky.

Norris, Edna, b. 1929. Athens County, Ohio.

Overbay, Druanna. Talbott, Tennessee.

Pinney, Clyde, b. 1930. Vinton County, Ohio.

Pinney, Lenora, b. 1929. Canoga, West Virginia.

Porter, Alta, b. 1917. Wise County, Virginia.

Porter, Lloyd Cecil, b. 1920. Wise County, Virginia.

Radwell, Crystal, b. 1980. Vinton County, Ohio.

Rathbourne, Mary, b. 1922. Vinton County, Ohio.

Rausch, Harold, b. 1927. Meigs County, Ohio

Rhea, Johnnie, b. 1931. Newman's Ridge, Hancock County, Tennessee.

Reinhart, Dulcie, b. 1918. Adams County, Ohio.

Rose, Wanda, b. 1932. Colburn, Kentucky.

Rouch, Mary, b. 1927. Meigs County, Ohio.

Shaffer, Ellen, b. 1919. Athens County, Ohio.

Shaffer, Henry, b. 1917. Athens County, Ohio.

Slades, Barbara, b. 1946. Franklin County, Ohio.

Smith, Dorothy, b. 1933. Athens County, Ohio.

Smith, Edger, b. 1920. Meigs County, Ohio.

Smith, Ken, b. 1945. Meigs County, Ohio.

Smith, Sarah, b. 1921. Marion County, Ohio.

Smith, Zelma, b. 1924. Vinton County, Ohio.

Sowers, Margaret, b. 1921. Perry County, Ohio.

Stallard, Sherynn. Wise, Virginia.

Stoneburger, Ida Mae, b. 1912. Athens County, Ohio.

Tabler, Dedra, b. 1964. Meigs County, Ohio.

Tabler, Margaret, b. 1931. Meigs County, Ohio.

Tabler, Winny, b. 1915. Meigs County, Ohio.

Thorpe, Cleland, b. 1940. Corbin, Kentucky.

Timberland, James, b. 1920. Vinton County, Ohio.

Tribe, Ivan. Vinton County, Ohio (Telephone interview).

Tucker, Alice Fanny, b. 1906. Nile, Tennessee.

Walker, Everett, b. 1918. Meigs County, Ohio.

Walker, Nancy Jean, b. 1950. Dandridge, Tennessee.

Weaver, Paul, b. 1929. Fairfield County, Ohio.

Wilson, Darlene. Putney, Kentucky.

Williams, John, b. 1926. Vinton County, Ohio.

Wills, Frances, b. 1921. Vinton County, Ohio.

Winkler, Wayne. Jonesborough, Tennessee.

Appendix B

Interview Outline

(The following was used as a guideline. I tried not to rely too heavily on my prepared questions and allowed the interviewee to follow any unexpected path he or she chose to take.)

Radio: Let's start by talking about your earliest memories of radio. (Before starting, please introduce yourselves and tell us where you grew up.)

How did you listen? (Did you sit around the radio with family or did you have it on while you worked or played? Was there some other way you listened?)

With whom did you listen? (Were you at home or at a neighbor's or relative's house?)

How has radio been important to your life? (Do you remember if it changed your daily routine or habits? If so, how?)

What did you listen to? What stations did you listen to?

How did you get your news?

What do you recall your parents listening to?

Electricity: How did it change your life?

What electrical appliances did you get after first getting electricity? Was radio the first purchase?

Television: (Same questions as with radio).

What can you remember as the difference between early radio and early television?

Internet: I'm interested in how people are using new technology.

Do you use the Internet? (If no, why not?)

What do you use it for? (Genealogy?)

When do you use it?

With whom do you use it?

Has it changed your daily routine?

Has it changed your life?

How did you get interested in the Internet? (Who got you interested?)

Where do you use it? (At home, work, library/public access?)

Do you have Internet access at home?

What sites do you visit? (Do you visit the Melungeon Web site?)

Do you consider yourself to be a Melungeon?

(This last question led to the examination of Melungeon identity construction.)

Bibliography

"All Day Long." *Newsweek*. 24 September 1951, 57.

Ancestry.com. http://www.ancestry.com.

Anderson, Benedict. *Imagined Communities: Reflections on the Origins and Spread of Nationalism*. New York: Verso, 1983.

Anzaldua, Gloria. "How to Tame a Wild Tongue." In *Out There: Marginalization and Contemporary Cultures*, edited by Russell Ferguson, Martha Gever, Trinh T. Minh-Ha, and Cornel West, 203–12. Cambridge: MIT Press, 1990.

Appalachian Regional Commission. "Newsroom: Legislative Update." http://www.arc.gov/index.do?nodeId=39 (accessed 24 May 2006).

Aston, Margaret. *The Fifteenth Century: The Prospect of Europe*. New York: Harcourt, Brace and World, 1968.

Aswell, James. "Lost Tribes of Tennessee's Mountains." *Nashville Banner*. 22 August 1937.

Azoulay, Katya Gibel. *Black, Jewish, and Interracial: It's Not the Color of Your Skin, but the Race of your Kin, & Other Myths of Identity*. Durham: Duke University Press, 1997.

Ball, Bonnie. *The Melungeon: Notes on the Origin of a Race*. Johnson City TN: The Overmountain Press, 1992.

Banks, Alan, Dwight Billings, and Karen Tice. "Appalachian Studies and Postmodernism." In *Multicultural Experiences, Multicultural Theories*, edited by Mary Rogers and George Ritzer, 80–91. New York: McGraw-Hill, 1996.

Banks, Dennis. "The Impact of Oral History on the Interviewer: A Study of Novice Historians." Paper presented at the annual meeting of the National Council for the Social Studies, Cincinnati, OH, 20–23 November 1997.

Barker, Chris. *Television, Globalization and Cultural Identities*. Philadelphia: Open University Press, 1999.

Batteau, Allen. *The Invention of Appalachia*. Tucson: The University of Arizona Press, 1990.

Baym, Nancy. "The Emergence of On-Line Community." In *Cybersociety 2.0: Revisiting Computer-Mediated Communication and Community*, edited by Steven Jones, 35–68. Thousand Oaks CA: Sage Publication, 1998.

Becker, Jane S. *Selling Tradition: Appalachia and the Construction of an American Folk, 1930–1940*. Chapel Hill: University of North Carolina Press, 1998.

Berger, Peter, and Thomas Luckmann. *The Social Construction of Reality: A Treatise in the Sociology of Knowledge*. New York: Doubleday, 1966.

Berry, Brewton. *Almost White*. New York: Macmillan, 1963.

Berry, Chad. *Southern Migrants, Northern Exiles*. Champaign: University of Illinois Press, 2000.

Bible, Jean Patterson. *Melungeons Yesterday and Today*. Jefferson City TN: Bible, 1975.

Bibliomania.com. http://bibliomania.com.

Billings, Dwight B., Gurney Norman, and Katherine Ledford, editors. *Confronting Appalachian Stereotypes: Back Talk from an American Region*. Lexington: University Press of Kentucky, 1999.

Branscome, James. "Annihilating the Hillbilly: The Appalachians' Struggle with America's Institution." *Katallagete* 3/2 (Winter 1971): 25–32.

Brodkin, Karen. *How Jews Became White Folks: And What That Says about Race in America*. New Brunswick NJ: Rutgers University Press, 1998.

Brooks, Tim, and Earle Marsh. *The Complete Directory to Prime Time Network TV Shows, 1946–Present*. New York: Ballantine Books, 1999.

Bruchac, Joseph. *Lasting Echoes: An Oral History of Native American People*. San Diego: Harcourt Brace and Co, 1997.

Cambiaire, Celestin Pierre. *Western Virginia Mountain Ballads, the Last Stand of American Pioneer Civilization*. London: The Mitre Press, 1935.

Campbell, Joseph. *The Power of Myth*. New York: Doubleday, 1988.

Carey, James. "Technology and Ideology: The Case of the Telegraph." *Prospects* 8 (1983): 303–25.

———. *Communication as Culture: Essays on Media and Society*. Boston: Unwin Hyman, 1989.

———. "The Roots of Modern Media Analysis." In *James Carey: A Critical Reader*, edited by Eve Stryker Munson and Catherine A. Warren, 34–59. Minneapolis: University of Minnesota Press, 1997.

Carter, Ginger. "WSB-TV, Atlanta: The Eyes of the South." In *Television in America: Local Station History from across the Nation*, edited by Michael Murray and Donald G. Godfrey, 79–105. Ames: Iowa State University Press, 1996.

Cattell-Gordon, David. "The Appalachian Inheritance: A Culturally Transmitted Traumatic Stress Syndrome?" *Journal of Progressive Human Services* 1/1 (1990): 41–57.

Caudill, Harry. *Night Comes to the Cumberlands, a Biography of a Depressed Area*. Boston: Little, Brown, 1963.

Clear Channel Communications, http://www.clearchannel.com/.

"Clear Tops for 20 Years," *Broadcasting*, 15 October 1962.

Clines, Francis X. "Fighting Appalachia's Top Cash Crop, Marijuana." *New York Times*, 28 February 2001, Kentucky edition, A10.

Collins, Carvel. "Nineteenth Century Fiction of the Southern Appalachians." *Bulletin of Bibliography* 17/1 (1942): 186–90.

Collins, P. H. "Learning from the Outsider Within: The Sociological Significance of Black Feminist Thought." In *(En)Gendering Knowledge: Feminists in Academe*, edited by Joan Hartman and Ellen Messer-Davidow, 40–65. Knoxville: The University of Tennessee Press, 1991.

Conquergood, Dwight. "Life in Big Red: Struggles and Accommodations in a Chicago Polyethnic Tenement." In *Structuring Diversity: Ethnographic Perspectives on the New Immigration*, edited by Louise Lamphere, 95–144. Chicago: University of Chicago Press, 1992.

Croteau, David, and William Hoynes. *Media Society: Industries, Images, and Audiences*. 3rd ed. Thousand Oaks: Pine Forge Press, 2003.

Crowe, Elizabeth. *Genealogy Online*. New York: McGraw-Hill, 2000.

Cunningham, Rodger. "Scotch-Irish and Others." *Appalachian Journal* 18/1 (Fall 1990): 84–90.

————. *Apples on the Flood: The Southern Mountain Experience.* Knoxville: University of Tennessee Press, 1987.

Curtis, Pavel. "Mudding: Social Phenomena in Text-Based Virtual Realities." In *Internet Dreams: Archetypes, Myths, and Metaphors,* edited by Mark Stefik, 265–92. Cambridge: MIT Press, 1996.

Cyndislist. http://www.cyndislist.com.

Darnton, Robert. "The Symbolic Elements of History." *The Journal of Modern History* 58/1 (March 1986): 218–34.

Davis, James. *Who Is Black? : One Nation's Definition.* University Park: Pennsylvania State University Press, 1991.

Davis, Louise. "The Mystery of the Melungeons." *Nashville Tennessean,* 22 September 1963.

Davis, Richard. *The Web of Politics: The Internet's Impact on the American Political System.* New York: Oxford University Press, 1999.

Deacon, Richard. *Madoc and the Discovery of America.* NY: George Braziller, 1966.

Deliverance, DVD. Directed by John Boorman. 1972; Burbank CA: Warner Home Video, 2004.

Derks, Scott, editor. *The Value of a Dollar: Prices and Incomes in the United States 1860–1989.* Detroit: Gale Research, 1994.

Deutsch, Karl, and William J. Foltz. *Nation-Building.* New York: Atherton Press, 1966.

Dewey, John. *Democracy and Education: An Introduction to the Philosophy of Education.* New York: The Macmillan Company, 1916.

Dickens, Arthur Geoffrey. *Reformation and Society in Sixteenth-Century Europe.* New York: Harcourt, Brace and World, 1966.

Dominick, Joseph. "Who Do You Think You Are? Personal Home Pages and Self-Presentation on the World Wide Web." *Journalism & Mass Communication Quarterly* 76/4 (December 1999): 646–58.

Douglas, Mary. *Purity and Danger: An Analysis of the Concepts of Pollution and Taboo.* London: Routledge, 1966.

Dromgoole, Will Allen. "The Malungeon Tree and Its Four Branches." *The Arena* 3 (June 1891): 470–79.

Dunaway, David, and Willa K. Baum. *Oral History: An Interdisciplinary Anthology.* Walnut Creek: Alta Mira Press, 1996.

Eisenstein, Elizabeth. *The Printing Press as an Agent of Change: Communications and Cultural Transformations in Early Modern Europe.* New York: Cambridge University Press, 1980.

Ellen, R. F., editor. *Ethnographic Research: A Guide to General Conduct.* London: Academic Press, 1992.

Eller, Ronald. *Miners, Millhands, and Mountaineers: Industrialization of the Appalachian South, 1880–1930.* Knoxville: University of Tennessee Press, 1982.

———. Foreword to *Confronting Appalachian Stereotypes: Back Talk from an American Region.* Edited by Dwight B. Billings, Gurney Norman, and Katherine Ledford. Lexington: University Press of Kentucky, 1999.

Encyclopedia of Appalachia. Knoxville: University of Tennessee Press, 2006.

Ergood, Bruce, and Bruce E. Kuhre, editors. *Appalachia: Social Context Past and Present,* 3rd ed. Dubuque IA: Kendall/Hunt Publishing Company, 1991.

Erickson, Hal. *Syndicated Television: The First Forty Years, 1947–1987.* Jefferson NC: McFarland, 1989.

Everett, C. S. "Melungeon History and Myth." *Appalachian Journal* 26/4 (Summer 1999): 358–409.

Fine, Michelle. "Working the Hyphens: Reinventing Self and Other in Qualitative Research." In *Handbook of Qualitative Research,* edited by Norman K. Denzin and Yvonna S. Lincoln, 70–82. Thousand Oaks: Sage Publications, 1994.

Fisher, Stephen L. *Fighting Back in Appalachia: Traditions of Resistance and Change.* Philadelphia: Temple University Press, 1993.

———. "Appalachian Stepchild." In *Confronting Appalachian Stereotypes: Back Talk from an American Region,* edited by Dwight B. Billings, Gurney Norman, and Katherine Ledford, 187–90. Lexington: University Press of Kentucky, 1999.

Fitzgerald, Thomas. "Media and Changing Metaphors of Ethnicity and Identity." *Media, Culture & Society* 13/2 (April 1991): 193–214.

Fleischman, Suzanne. "Gender, the Personal and the Voice of Scholarship: A Viewpoint." *Signs: Journal of Women in Culture and Society* 23/4 (Summer 1998): 975–1016.

Forsyth, Howard. "The Radio and Rural Research." *Rural Sociology* 4/1 (March 1939): 67–77.

Foust, James. "A History of the Clear Channel Broadcasting Service, 1934–1980." Ph.D. dissertation, Ohio University, 1994.

Fox, John, Jr. *The Kentuckians.* New York: C. Scribner's Sons, 1898.

———. *The Trail of the Lonesome Pine.* New York: Harper and Brothers Publishers, 1908.

Friend, Tad. "White Hot Trash." *New York Magazine,* 22 August 1994, 23-29.

Frisch, Michael. *A Shared Authority: Essays on the Craft and Meaning of Oral and Public History.* Albany: State University of New York Press, 1990.

Frost, William Goodell. "Our Contemporary Ancestors in the Southern Mountains." *Atlantic Monthly,* 83 (1899), 311-19.

Fürsich, Elfriede, and Melinda Robins. "Africa.com: The Self-Representation of Sub-Saharan Nations on the World Wide Web." *Critical Studies in Mass Communication* 19/2 (June 2002): 190–211.

Gaines, Brian R., and Mildred L. G. Shaw. "Human-Computer Interaction in Online Communities." *Journal of Research and Practice in Information Technology* 33/1 (2001): 3–15.

Garrett, Betty. "An Appalachian Author Describes His Life Style." *Appalachia* 6/3 (December/January 1972–73): 24–28.

Gates, Bill. *The Road Ahead.* New York: Viking, 1996.

———. *Business @ the Speed of Thought: Using a Digital Nervous System.* With Collins Hemingway. New York: Warner Books, 1999.

Gianakos, Larry. *Television Drama Series Programming: A Comprehensive Chronicle, 1947–1959.* Metuchen NJ: Scarecrow Press, 1980.

Gillespie, Richard. *Manufacturing Knowledge: A History of the Hawthorne Experiments.* New York: Cambridge University Press, 1991.

Gluck, Sherna Berger, and Daphne Patai. *Women's Words: The Feminist Practice of Oral History.* New York: Routledge, 1991.

Gordon, Cyrus. *Before Columbus.* NY: Crown Publishers, 1971.

Gordon, Lois, and Alan Gordon. *American Chronicle: Seven Decades in American Life 1920–1989*. New York: Crown Publisher, 1990.

Gould, Jack. "TV Transforming U.S. Social Scene: Challenges Films." *The New York Times*, 24 June 1951, 1.

Griffin, Larry J., and Ashley B. Thompson. "Appalachia and the South: Collective Memory, Identity, and Representation." *Appalachian Journal* 29/3 (Spring 2002): 296–327.

Guy, Roger. "Down Home: Perception and Reality Among Southern White Migrants in Post World War II Chicago." *The Oral History Review* 24/2 (December 1997): 35–52.

Habermas, Jurgen. "The Public Sphere." In *Jurgen Habermas On Society and Politics: A Reader*, edited by Steven Seidman, 231–36. Boston: Beacon Press, 1989.

Hafner, Katie. *The Well: A Story of Love, Death, and Real Life in the Seminal Online Community*. New York: Carroll and Graf, 2001.

Hall, Stuart. "Who Needs Identity?" In *Questions of Cultural Identity*, edited by Stuart Hall and P. Du Gay, 1–17. London: Sage, 1996.

Hamersley, Martin, and Paul Atkinson. *Ethnography: Principle in Practice*. London: Tavistock, 1983.

Harkins, Anthony A. "The Hillbilly in the Living Room: Television Representations of Southern Mountaineers in Situation Comedies, 1952-1971." *Appalachian Journal* 29/1-2 (Fall/Winter 2001-02): 98-126.

———. *Hillbilly: A Cultural History of an American Icon*. New York: Oxford University Press, 2004.

Harney, Will Wallace. "A Strange Land and Peculiar People." *Lippincott's Magazine* 12/31 (October 1873), 429–38.

Hay, George. *Story of the Grand Ole Opry*. Nashville: Hay, 1953.

Head, Sydney, Christopher H. Sterling, and Lemuel B. Schofield. *Broadcasting in America: A Survey of Electronic Media*. Boston: Houghton Mifflin, 1994.

Henige, David. "Brent Kennedy's Melungeons." *Appalachian Journal* 25/3 (Spring 1998): 270–86.

Hill, Kevin A., and John E. Hughes. *Cyberpolitics: Citizen Activism in the Age of the Internet*. Lanham MD: Rowman & Littlefield, 1998.

Hilmes, Michele. *Radio Voices: American Broadcasting, 1922–1952.* Minneapolis: University of Minnesota Press, 1997.

Hobson, Fred. "Up in the Country." In *Confronting Appalachian Stereotypes: Back Talk from an American Region,* edited by Dwight B. Billings, Gurney Norman, and Katherine Ledford, 174–86. Lexington: University Press of Kentucky, 1999.

Hogg, Michael, Deborah J. Terry, and Katherine M. White. "A Tale of Two Theories: A Critical Comparison of Identity Theory with Social Identity Theory." *Social Psychology Quarterly* 58 (December 1995): 255–69.

Hollinger, David. *Postethnic America: Beyond Multiculturalism.* New York: BasicBooks, 1995.

Holmes, David, editor. *Virtual Politics: Identity and Community in Cyberspace.* London: Sage, 1997.

Ivey, Saundra Keyes. "Oral, Printed, and Popular Culture Traditions Related to the Melungeons of Hancock County, Tennessee." Ph.D. dissertation, Indiana University, 1976.

Johnson, Mattie Ruth. *My Melungeon Heritage: A Story of Life on Newman's Ridge.* Johnson City TN: Overmountain Press, 1997.

Johnson, Steven. *Interface Culture: How New Technology Transforms the Way We Create and Communicate.* San Francisco: Harper Edge, 1997.

Jones, Steven. "Understanding Community in the Information Age." In *Cybersociety: Computer-Mediated Communication and Community,* edited by Steven Jones, 10–35. Thousand Oaks CA: Sage Publications, 1995.

———. *Cybersociety 2.0: Revisiting Computer-Mediated Communication and Community.* Thousand Oaks CA: Sage, 1998.

Keller, Kenneth. "What Is Distinctive About the Scotch-Irish?" In *Appalachian Frontiers: Settlement, Society, & Development in the Preindustrial Era,* edited by Robert Mitchell, 69–86. Lexington: University Press of Kentucky, 1991.

Kennedy, N. Brent, and Robyn Vaughan Kennedy. *The Melungeons: The Resurrection of a Proud People: An Untold Story of Ethnic Cleansing in America.* Macon GA: Mercer University Press, 1997.

Kim, Amy Jo. *Community Building on the Web*. Berkeley CA: Peachpit Press, 2000.

Kipling, Rudyard. "The English Flag." In *Extravagant Strangers: A Literature of Belonging*, edited by Caryl Phillips, 36–40. Boston: Faber and Faber, 1997.

Kirkwood, James, and Nicholas Dante. *A Chorus Line*. New York: Applause. 1975.

Klotter, James. "The Black South and White Appalachia." *Journal of American History* 66/4 (March 1980): 832–49.

Kolko, Beth, and Elizabeth Reid. "Dissolution and Fragmentation: Problems in Online Communities." In *Cybersociety 2.0: Revisiting Computer-Mediated Communication and Community*, edited by Steven Jones, 212–29. Thousand Oaks CA: Sage Press, 1998.

Lamb, Terri. *E-genealogy: Finding Your Family Roots Online*. Indianapolis: Sams, 2000.

Larson, Charles. *Persuasion: Reception and Responsibility*. Belmont CA: Wadsworth, 1992.

Lee, Alfred McClung. *The Daily Newspaper in America: The Evolution of a Social Instrument*. New York: The Macmillan Company, 1937.

Lewis, Ronald. "Beyond Isolation and Homogeneity: Diversity and the History of Appalachia." In *Confronting Appalachian Stereotypes: Back Talk from an American Region*, edited by Dwight B. Billings, Gurney Norman, and Katherine Ledford, 21–46. Lexington: University Press of Kentucky. 1999.

Lindlof, Thomas R. *Qualitative Communication Research Methods*. Thousand Oaks CA: Sage Publications, 1995.

Loftus, Elizabeth. "Tricked by Memory." In *Memory and History: Essays on Recalling and Interpreting Experience*, edited by Jaclyn Jeffrey and Glenace Edwall, 17–32. New York: University Press of America, 1994.

Lowe, Janet. *Bill Gates Speaks: Insight from the World's Greatest Entrepreneur*. New York: John Wiley & Sons, 1998.

Lowenthal, David. *The Past Is a Foreign Country*. Cambridge: Oxford Press, 1985.

Lull, James. "The Social Uses of Television." *Human Communication Research* 6/3 (Spring 1980): 197–209.

Lynch, Michael. "Against Reflexivity as an Academic Virtue and Source of Privileged Knowledge." *Theory, Culture & Society* 17/3 (June 2000): 26–54.

MacDonald, J. Fred. *Don't Touch that Dial! Radio Programming in American Life, 1920–1960*. Chicago: Nelson-Hall, 1979.

Maggard, Sally. "Cultural Hegemony: The News Media and Appalachia." *Appalachian Journal* 12/3 (Autumn/Winter 1984-85): 67–83.

Malone, Bill. *Country Music, U.S.A.* Austin: University of Texas Press, 1985.

Mascia-Lees, Frances. "The Postmodernist Turn in Anthropology: Cautions from a Feminist Perspective." *Signs* 15/1 (Autumn 1989): 7–33.

McGlothlen, Mike. *Melungeons and other Mestee Groups*. Gainesville FL: Mike McGlothlen, 1994.

McKenna, Katelyn Y. A., and John A. Bargh. "Coming out in the Age of the Internet: Identity 'Demarginalization' through Virtual Group Participation." *Journal of Personality and Social Psychology* 75/3 (September 1998): 681–94.

McLuhan, Marshall. *Understanding Media: The Extensions of Man*. New York: McGraw-Hill, 1964.

Melody, William. "On the Political Economy of Communication in the Information Society." In *Illuminating the Blindspots: Essays Honoring Dallas W. Symthe*, edited by Dallas Smythe, Janet Wasko, Vincent Mosco, and Manjunath Pendakur, 63–81. Norwood NJ: Ablex Pub. Corp., 1993.

Melungeon Web site. http://www.melungeon.org.

Mendelsohn, Harold. "Listening to Radio." In *People, Society, and Mass Communications*, edited by Lewis Dexter and David White, 239–49. New York: Free Press of Glencoe, 1964.

Miller, Daniel, and Don Slater. *The Internet: An Ethnographic Approach*. Oxford: Berg, 2000.

Mitra, Ananda. "Diasporic Websites: Ingroup and Outgroup Discourse." *Critical Studies in Mass Communication* 14/2 (June 1997): 158–81.

Mohammed, Shaheed. "Self-Presentation of Small Developing Countries on the World Wide Web: A Study of Official Websites." *New Media & Society* 6/4 (August 2004): 469–86.

Mosco, Vincent. *The Political Economy of Communication: Rethinking and Renewal.* Thousand Oaks CA: Sage Publications, 1996.

Mosco, Vincent, and Vanda Rideout. "Media Policy in North America." In *International Media Research: A Critical Survey,* edited by John Corner, Philip Schlesinger, and Roger Silverstone, 154–83. London: Routledge, 1997.

Mountain Vision: Homegrown Television in Appalachia, videocassette. Directed by Susan Wehling and Jeff Hawkins. Whitesburg KY: Appalshop, 1990.

Murray, Michael, and Donald G. Godfrey, editors. *Television in America: Local Station History from across the Nation.* Ames: Iowa State University Press, 1996.

National Telecommunications & Information Administration. "Falling through the Net: New Commerce Report Shows Dramatic Growth in Number of Americans Connected to Internet." *U.S. Department of Commerce News,* 8 July 1999. http://www.ntia.doc.gov/ntiahome/press/fttn070899.htm.

Negroponte, Nicholas. *Being Digital.* New York: Alfred Knopf, 1995.

Nelson, Jenny. "Phenomenology as Feminist Methodology: Explicating Interviews." In *Doing Research on Women's Communication: Perspectives on Theory and Method,* edited by Kathryn Carter and Carole Spitzack, 221–41. Norwood NJ: Ablex Pub. Corp., 1989.

Newcomb, Horace. "Appalachia on Television: Region as Symbol of American Popular Culture." *Appalachian Journal* 7/1–2 (Autumn/Winter 1979-80): 155–64.

Norris, Pippa. *Digital Divide: Civic Engagement, Information, Poverty, and the Internet Worldwide.* Cambridge, UK: Cambridge University Press, 2001.

Nyden, Paul. *Black Coal Miners in the United States.* New York: The American Institute for Marxist Studies, 1974.

Ohio Rural Electric Cooperatives. *The Light and the Power: Commemorating 50 Years of Electricity in Rural Ohio.* Columbus: Ohio Rural Electric Cooperatives, Inc, 1985.

Olorunnisola, Anthony, A. "Radio and African Rural Communities: Structural Strategies for Social Mobilization." *Journal of Radio Studies* 4 (1997): 242–52.

Ong, Walter. *Rhetoric, Romance, and Technology: Studies in the Interaction of Expression and Culture.* Ithaca NY: Cornell University Press, 1971.

———. *Orality and Literacy: The Technologizing of the Word.* London: Metheun, 1982.

Pacey, Arnold. *The Culture of Technology.* Cambridge MA: The MIT Press, 1994.

Parker, Edwin E., and Heather E. Hudson. *Electronic Byways: State Policies for Rural Development through Telecommunications.* Boulder: Westview Press, 1992.

Podber, Jacob J. "Early Radio in Rural Appalachia: An Oral History." *Journal of Radio Studies* 8/2 (Winter 2001): 388–410.

———. "Radio's Early Arrival in Appalachia: A Harbinger of the Global Society." In *Global Media Studies: Ethnographic Perspectives*, edited by Patrick D. Murphy and Marwan M. Kraidy, 184–212. New York: Routledge Press, 2003.

———. "The Debut of Broadcasting in Small Town America: A Reflection of Community Radio throughout the World." *Global Media Journal* 3/4 (Spring 2004), http://lass.calumet.purdue.edu/cca/gmj/sp04/gmj-sp04-podber.htm

Poindexter, Mark. "Radio in Paris: Can Community Stations Survive?" *Journal of Radio Studies* 4 (1997): 253–68.

Portelli, Alessandro. *The Death of Luigi Trastulli, and Other Stories: Form and Meaning in Oral History.* Albany: State University of New York Press, 1991.

Postman, Neil. *Technopoly: The Surrender of Culture to Technology.* New York: Vintage Books, 1993.

Postman, Neil, and Camille Paglia, "Two Cultures—Television versus Print." In *Communication in History: Technology, Culture*, Society, edited by David Crowley and Paul Heyer, 288–300. New York: Longman, 1999.

Preece, Jenny. "Sociability and Usability in Online Communities: Determining and Measuring Success." *Behaviour and Information Technology* 20/5 (2001): 347–56.

Price, Edward. "The Melungeons: A Mixed-Blood Strain of the Southern Appalachians." *The Geographical Review* 41/2 (April 1951): 256–71.

Project Gutenberg. http://www.gutenberg.org.

Rabinow, Paul. *Reflections on Fieldwork in Morocco*. Berkeley: University of California Press, 1977.

Raitz, Karl, and Richard Ulack. "Regional Definitions." In *Appalachia: Social Context Past and Present*, edited by Bruce Ergood and Bruce Kuhre, 10–25. Dubuque: Kendall/Hunt Publishing Company, 1991.

Rehder, John, B. "The Scotch-Irish and English in Appalachia." In *To Build in a New Land: Ethnic Landscapes in North America*, edited by Allen Noble, 95–118. Baltimore: The Johns Hopkins University Press, 1992.

Rheingold, Howard. *The Virtual Community: Homesteading on the Electronic Frontier*. Reading MA: Addison-Wesley, 1993.

———. *Smart Mobs: The Next Social Revolution*. Cambridge MA: Perseus, 2002.

Riesman, David. *The Lonely Crowd: A Study of the Changing American Character*. New Haven: Yale University Press, 1950.

Riney-Kehrberg, Pamela. "The Radio Diary of Mary Dyck, 1936–1955: The Listening Habits of a Kansas Farm Woman." *Journal of Radio Studies* 5/2 (Summer 1998): 66–79.

Ritchie, Donald A. Foreword to *Memory and History: Essays on Recalling and Interpreting Experience*, edited by Jaclyn Jeffrey and Glenace Edwall, v-xi. New York: University Press of America. 1994.

———. *Doing Oral History*. New York: Twayne Publishers, 1995.

Rockwell, Rick. "Finding Power of Hidden Radio Audiences in the Fields of Guatemala." *Journal of Radio Studies* 8/2 (Winter 2001): 425–41.

Rodriguez, Richard. *Hunger of Memory: The Education of Richard Rodriguez: An Autobiography.* Boston: D. R. Godine, 1982.

Rootsweb. http://www.rootsweb.com.

Salisbury, Morse. "Radio and Country Life." *Rural America* 14/2 (February 1936): 17–18.

Salstrom, Paul. *Appalachia's Path to Dependency: Rethinking a Region's Economic History, 1730–1940.* Lexington: University Press of Kentucky, 1994.

Shackelford, Laurel, and Bill Weinberg, editors. *Our Appalachia.* New York: Hill and Wang, 1977.

Shaffir, William, and Robert A. Stebbins, editors. *Experiencing Fieldwork: An Inside View of Qualitative Research.* Newbury Park: Sage Publications, 1991.

Shannon, Robert, editor and annotator. *Annotated Constitution of Tennessee.* Nashville: State of Tennessee, 1915.

Shapiro, Henry. *Appalachia on Our Mind: The Southern Mountains and Mountaineers in the American Consciousness, 1870–1920.* Chapel Hill: The University of North Carolina Press, 1978.

Shepherd, Lewis. "What Do You Know about The Melungeons?" *Nashville Banner,* 3 August 1924, 88.

Silver, David, "Margins in the Wires: Looking for Race, Gender, and Sexuality in the Blacksburg Electronic Village." In *Race in Cyberspace,* edited by Beth E. Kolko et al., 133–50. New York: Routledge, 2000.

———. "Selling Cyberspace: Constructing and Deconstructing the Rhetoric of Community," *Southern Communication Journal* 70/3 (Spring 2005): 187–99.

Smith, Herb, E. *Strangers and Kin,* videocassette. Directed by Herb E. Smith. Whitesburg KY: Appalshop, 1984.

Smulyan, Susan. *Selling Radio: The Commercialization of American Broadcasting 1920–1934.* Washington: Smithsonian Institution Press, 1994.

Smythe, Dallas Walker. "After Bicycles, What?" In *Counterclockwise: Perspectives on Communication,* edited by Thomas Guback, 230–44. Boulder: Westview Press, 1994.

Snyder, Bob. "Image and Identity in Appalachia." *Appalachian Journal* 9/2 (Winter/Spring 1982): 124–33.

Sontag, Susan. *On Photography*. New York: Farrar, Straus and Giroux, 1977.

Sovine, Melanie Lou. "The Mysterious Melungeons: A Critique of Mythical Image." Ph.D. dissertation, University of Kentucky, 1982.

Spigel, Lynn. "The Domestic Economy of Television Viewing in Postwar America." *Critical Studies in Mass Communication* 6/4 (December 1989): 337–54.

Sproull, Lee, and Samer Faraj. "Some Consequences of Electronic Groups." In *Internet Dreams: Archetypes, Myths, and Metaphors*, edited by Mark Stefik, 125–34. Cambridge: MIT Press, 1996.

Stacey, Judith. "Can There Be a Feminist Ethnography?" In *Women's Words: The Feminist Practice of Oral History*, edited by Sherna Berger Gluck and Daphne Patai, 111–20. New York: Routledge, 1991.

Stefik, Mark, editor. *Internet Dreams: Archetypes, Myths, and Metaphors*. Cambridge: MIT Press, 1996.

Stephens, Lowndes. "Media Exposure and Modernization among the Appalachian Poor." *Journalism Quarterly* 49/2 (Summer 1972): 247–57.

Sterling, Christopher, and John Kittross. *Stay Tuned: A Concise History of American Broadcasting*. Belmont CA: Wadsworth Publishing Co, 1990.

Sultana, Ronald. "Ethnography and the Politics of Absence." In *Critical Theory and Educational Research*, edited by Peter McLaren and James Giarelli, 113–25, Albany: State University of New York Press, 1995.

Thompson, Paul Richard. *The Voice of the Past: Oral History*. Oxford: Oxford University Press, 1978.

Turkle, Sherry. "Virtuality and Its Discontents." *The American Prospect* 7/24 (Winter 1996): 50–57.

Turner, William Hobart, and Edward J. Cabbell. *Blacks in Appalachia*. Lexington: University Press of Kentucky, 1985.

Tyler, Stephen, A. "Post-Modern Ethnography: From Document of the Occult to Occult Document." In *Writing Culture: The Poetics and*

Politics of Ethnography, edited by James Clifford and George E. Marcus, 122–40. Berkeley: University of California Press, 1986.

Ulack, Richard, and Karl Raitz. "Appalachia: A Comparison of the Cognitive and Appalachian Regional Commission Regions." *Southeastern Geographer* 21/1 (May 1981): 40–53.

US Bureau of the Census. *Sixteenth Census of the United States: 1943 Housing—Volume II. General Characteristics.* Washington DC: United States Government Printing Office, 1940.

US Bureau of the Census. *Census of Housing: 1950.* Taken as part of the Seventeenth Decennial Census of the United States. Volume I—General Characteristics, Part 5. Washington DC: United States Government Printing Office, 1953.

Whisnant, David. "Ethnicity and the Recovery of Regional Identity in Appalachia: Thoughts upon Entering the Zone of Occult Instability." *Soundings* 56/1 (Spring 1973): 124–38.

———. *Modernizing the Mountaineer: People, Power, and Planning in Appalachia.* New York: Burt Franklin, 1980.

White, William Allen. *A Puritan in Babylon, the Story of Calvin Coolidge.* New York: The Macmillan Company, 1938.

Wilbur, Shawn. "An Archaeology of Cyberspaces: Virtuality, Community, Identity." In *Internet Culture*, edited by David Porter, 5–22. New York: Routledge, 1997.

Wilkinson, Crystal. "On Being 'Country': One Affrilachian Woman's Return Home," In *Confronting Appalachian Stereotypes: Back Talk from an American Region*, edited by Dwight B. Billings, Gurney Norman, and Katherine Ledford, 184–86. Lexington: University Press of Kentucky, 1999.

Williamson, Jerry Wayne. *Southern Mountaineers in Silent Films: Plot Synopses of Movies about Moonshining, Feuding, and Other Mountain Topics, 1904–1929.* Jefferson NC: McFarland, 1994.

———. *Hillbillyland: What the Movies Did to the Mountains and What the Mountains Did to the Movies.* Chapel Hill: University of North Carolina Press, 1995.

Woal, Michael, and Linda Woal. "Forgotten Pioneer: Philco's WPTZ, Philadelphia." In *Television in America: Local Station History from across the Nation*, edited by Michael Murray and Donald G. Godfrey, 39–60. Ames: Iowa State University Press, 1996.

Wray, Matt, and Annalee Newitz. *White Trash: Race and Class in America.* New York: Routledge, 1997.

Wright, Lawrence. "One Drop of Blood." *New Yorker.* 25 July 1994, 47.

Yarrow, Mike. "Voices from the Coalfields." In *Communities in Economic Crisis: Appalachia and the South*, edited by John Gaventa, Barbara E. Smith, and Alex W. Willingham, 38–52. Philadelphia: Temple University Press, 1990.

Yow, Valerie. "Do I Like Them Too Much?: Effects of the Oral History Interview on the Interviewer and Vice-Versa." *The Oral History Review* 24/1 (Summer 1997): 55–79.

Zelinsky, Wilbur. *The Cultural Geography of the United States.* Englewood Cliffs: Prentice-Hall, 1973.

Index

NTIA. *See* National
Telecommunications and
Information Administration
(NTIA)

Ohio Rural Electric Cooperatives, 70
one-drop rule, 50, 51
Ong, Walter, 20, 69
on-line communities. *See* virtual
communities
oral historians, 21–22, 26, 63
oral history, 20, 23, 63–64
oral history interviews: analysis of,
27–29; challenges of, 21–22;
geographic locations of, 38; give
and take in, 27; questions in,
28–29; snowball effect, 22–23;
spontaneous, 24–25, 61–62; story
circle in, 23–24; tape recorders in,
20–21, 27
oral sources, 29, 62–63, 135–137. *See
also individual names*
oral tradition, of Catholics, 13
otherness: Appalachians and, 40;
author and, 8–9; hipness of, 5–6;
of Melungeons, 45, 49, 54
Ozzie and Harriet show, The (radio
and television show), 103

Pacey, Arnold, 114
Paley, William, 102–103
paper affordability, and mass-
produced books, 14
Paris radio stations, 131
Parker, Edwin B., 17, 18
Parton, Dolly, 107
Patai, Daphne, 8
photography, 21
Pinney, Clyde, 68, 73, 85–86,
101–102
Pinney, Lenora, 81, 84
Plato, on politically responsible cities,
12

point of view, of unprivileged, 20
Popular Mechanics (magazine), 67
Portelli, Alessandro, 62–64
Porter, Alta, 54–55
Porter, Emmett, 97
Porter, Lloyd, 54–55, 82–83, 90–91,
97
Portuguese ancestry, of Melungeons,
49
Postman, Neil, 12, 114
printing press invention, 13
prizefights, 78, 81–82
Protestants, and the "word," 13
public sphere, concept of, 126

racial slurs, 30, 57
radio: affordability of, 91–92; arrival
of, in Appalachia, 2–3, 14;
battery-powered, 70–73; and
broadened horizons, 85–86, 102;
clear channel stations, 73–76; and
community cohesion, 79–83,
130–131; console sets, 69; crystal
sets with earphones, 67–68;
dancing to, 76, 82–83; electric
sets, 73; and housework, 84–85;
low-power FM stations (LPFM),
74, 131–132; news programming,
77–78; ownership of, in
Appalachia, 66–67; programming,
and benefits to television,
101–102; and secondary orality,
20; and sporting events, 78;
transition from, to television,
102–104; tube sets, 68; variety
shows, 77; Web radio, 132–133.
See also soap operas; *specific
programs*
radio talent raids, 102–103
Raitz, Karl, 37–38
ramps and "ramps," 54
reflexivity, in participant-observation,
5–7

tobacco, 95–96
transcripts, use of, 27–28
Tribe, Ivan, 76
tube radio sets, 68
Tunney, Gene, 78
Turkle, Sherry, 114–115, 121
TV-stove, 92

UHF channels, 88–89
Ulack, Richard, 37–38
Unions (of Melungeons). *See*
  Melungeon Heritage Association
Upland South, 38
U.S. census (1940), 70–71
US Airways, 124–125

variety shows, 77
vernacular, the, as context
  information, 28
VHF channels, 88–89
videotape use in group interviews, 23,
  27
videotex, 110
Vinton County, Ohio, 70
virtual communities: AOL and, 15;
  construction of, 117–120;
  evolution of, to face-to-face,
  114–115, 121–122; the Internet
  and, 111–115; visiting with
  friends of, 123–124

Walker, Nancy J., 95
Waters, John, 30
WBAP radio station, Fort Worth, 76
Weaver, Paul, 67
Web radio, 132–133
Webb, Cecil, 75
Weekly Reader (newspaper for school
  children), 89
Western-Holly Company, 92
westerns, 104
Wheeling Jamboree (radio program),
  77

Whisnant, David, 37, 45
whiteness, 40
Wilbur, Shawn, 112
Williams, John, 72, 77–78
Williamson, Jerry Wayne, 4, 40, 107
Wilson, Darlene, 41, 58, 117–118,
  121
windmill-powered batteries, 72
Winkler, Wayne, 122
WLS National Barn Dance, 76, 77
WLS radio station, Chicago, 76
WLW Barn Dance, 77
WLW radio station, Cincinnati, 76,
  103
World Trade Organization protests
  (1999), 129
World War II, 74, 78, 81, 88
World Wide Web. *See* Internet
Wray, Matt, 40
wrestling programs, on television,
  98–99
written communication, control of,
  13
written sources, reliability of, 63
WSB radio station, Atlanta, 75, 76
WSM Barn Dance (radio program), 76
WSM radio station, Nashville, 76
Wynn, Ed, 103

Yiddish language, 9
Yow, Valerie, 11, 26

Zelinsky, Wilbur, 38